Sarasota Sister Cities
Sixty Years of Citizen Diplomacy

Craig H. Hullinger & Raymond A. Young

Contents

Prologue

The Sister Cities Association of Sarasota (SCAS) is celebrating 60 years since the founding in 1963. We have served on the board of directors of SCAS for many years and felt it was time to record the great achievements realized by the organization during the past sixty years. In this treatise we recognize significant exchanges, events and activities that have been carried out over the years and also recognize the many volunteers that have dedicated their valuable time in service to SCAS.

The book will also serve those interested in how a mid-size city manages sister city relationships around the world. Our organizational structure is described as well as the functions of all the board members, including the Vice Presidents and the Directors for each of the sister cities. SCAS also serves the general Sarasota community with the public invited to all our luncheons, wide ranging presentations and celebratory events. The premier "One World Award," conceived by board member Bill Wallace, annually honors one remarkable individual and one outstanding organization in our community that has enhanced "Understanding and Respect" among citizens of the world through their extraordinary work or volunteer service.

The information provided in the book provides a template for cities contemplating the development of their own sister city program and contains useful ideas for possible new programs, events and exchanges in other sister city organizations.

Many SCAS members assisted in preparation of this book and we give special thanks to SCAS past presidents Bill Wallace, Linda Rosenbluth, Hope Byrnes, Carla Rayman, Tom Halbert, Beth Ruyle, Toni Duval and Miriam Kramer as well as board members Sue Gordon, Gayle Maxey, Fred Bloom, Kenney DeCamp, Pauline Mitchel, Grisell Aleman, Isabelle Eidet and David Harralson. We are also indebted to Judy Caldwell-Moore our SCAS historian who accumulated many news articles, pictures and newsletters over the years that made it possible to produce this book about our sixty year history. All proceeds from the book are donated to SCAS.

Introduction

Sister City International (SCI) began in Washington, D.C. in 1956 during the United States presidency of Dwight D. Eisenhower. Eisenhower was the Allied Supreme Commander of the armies of Europe during World War II. He viewed the horrific devastation of human life and property resulting from that tragic time in world history. He thought there must be a better way to a lasting peace – trying "citizen diplomacy" rather than "governmental diplomacy" the latter of which unfortunately resulted in continuing conflicts over the many centuries of humankind. "Citizen diplomacy" in Eisenhower's way of thinking was an actual "eyeball to eyeball" interfacing of everyday citizens, meeting personally on each other's "turf" (in the U.S. and overseas). Thereby learning how they lived, carried on their daily lives and overcame whatever challenges they faced. It was envisioned that this would bring about enhanced understanding and respect for all global citizens. It was felt that this could be accomplished through exchanges (visitations) of citizens engaged in the arts, business, civic activities, service clubs (Rotary, Kiwanis, boy/girl scouts, etc), education, sports and government.

SCAS former VP-Education Ray Young visited the Eisenhower Library in Abilene, Kansas that documents the path to peace through citizen diplomacy after WWII.

The national SCI organization has a membership of 545 sister cities with 2,121 partnerships in 145 countries on six continents. SCI bestows awards to sister city organizations in the USA that have carried out significant and unique exchanges and SCAS has been the recipient of several of these awards over the years.

All sizes of communities have sister cities around the world from villages in northern Minnesota partnering with similar communities in Scandinavia to huge cities such as New York and Los Angles twining with major international cities around the world. Sarasota falls in the mid-range of the city sizes.

Sarasota

Sarasota is a city with a population of about 55,000 in Sarasota county that has about 450,000 people. The city is located on beautiful Sarasota Bay inland from a series of barrier islands that contain award winning beaches on the Gulf of Mexico. It is a very attractive and popular tourist destination not only for the beaches but also for many cultural offerings as well. The performing arts include Sarasota Ballet, Sarasota Opera, Asolo Repertory Theater, Florida Studio Theater and the Van Wezel Performing Arts Hall. The world class John and Mable Ringling Museum of Art displays the works of some of the most famous artists through the centuries.

Ringling Museum Mansion in Sarasota

The Marie Selby Botanical Garden in Sarasota contains a wide range of tropical plants and is known for the extensive collections of bromeliads and orchids. The Mote Marine Laboratory & Aquarium exhibits a broad array of marine life and the staff carry out research on many aspects of marine animals and environment. Manatee, shark and turtle conservation and rescue, and marine environmental health and ecology are just few of the programs at the laboratory.

The Selby Botanical Garden is known for the beautiful displays
of orchids and bromeliads

There are several institutions of higher learning in Sarasota including the University of South Florida-Sarasota/Manatee, Ringling College of Art & Design, State College of Florida and New College of Florida. Florida State University in consort with the Asolo Conservatory in Sarasota offers specialized actor training.

Golf and rowing are notable sports activities in the area and numerous national and world rowing championships are held at the Nathan Benderson facility in the region.

Rowing competition at Nathan Benderson Park

Sister Cities Association of Sarasota
Creating a Path to Peace

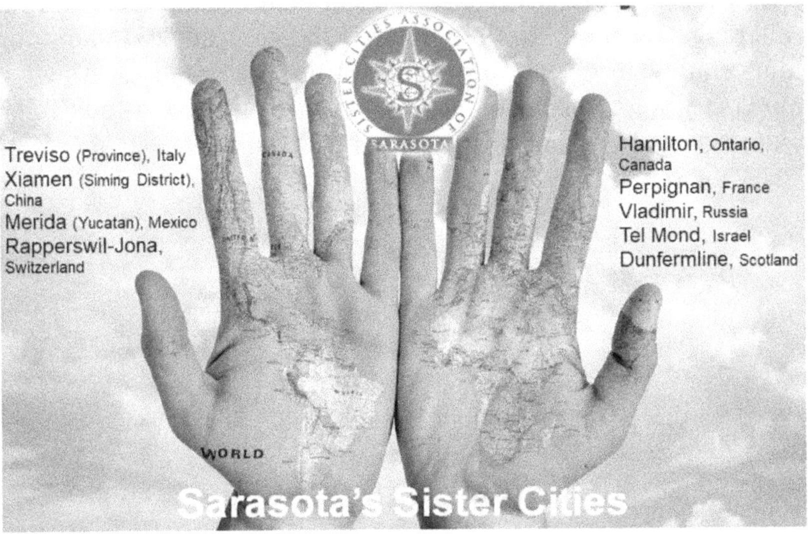

The Sister Cities Association of Sarasota (SCAS) was founded in 1963 and has served our community and international partners in this 60 years. SCAS is an all-volunteer non-profit institution dedicated to promoting peace and understanding in the world. Our organization is a member of the broader Sister Cities International program.

SCAS is an independent organization that partners with the City of Sarasota to strengthen our international relationships with our Sister Cities. We promote peace by fostering citizen diplomacy through exchanges and projects between Sarasota and our Sister Cities in the areas of culture, education, tourism, sports, business and government. The objective of SCAS is to foster international relationships between Sarasota and international cities that have similar interests by creating exchanges in areas of culture, education, tourism, sports, business and government.

The concept of the international network of Sister Cities began in response to President Dwight D. Eisenhower's vision to enhance worldwide peace and understanding one handshake at a time. Sarasota's citizen diplomats are involved in numerous sister city outreach programs to build bridges and enhance worldwide peace and understanding.

Sarasota Sister Cities receives partial support from the City of Sarasota to assist our extensive international exchanges. The city also provides office space for our organization in the historic Federal Building located in downtown Sarasota.

In this 60th year of service, Sarasota Sister Cities continues to plan and administer numerous programs to promote world peace among our Sister Cities' citizens. We work with our partners to further "citizen diplomacy," creating and maintaining personal relationships that are vital to furthering better relationships around the world. Our members are proud of their efforts, and continue with activities that help to improve our relationships with our friends in our Sister Cities. As we complete our 60th anniversary we can be proud of our past activities and look forward to many more interactions with our international friends.

 **Mission Statement** 

The mission of the Sister Cities Association of Sarasota, Inc. is to develop respect, understanding and cooperation one individual, one community at a time.

To accomplish this mission we develop relationships with people in our twinned cities that have interests and environments similar to those in Sarasota. Working outside the realm of government, but with its support, we maintain a special focus on areas with significant opportunities to facilitate cultural and educational exchanges, economic partnerships, increased tourism and humanitarian assistance.

Our Sister Cities

Sister Cities for Sarasota have generally been selected based on their similar size and cultural and educational offerings. For selection of a new sister city, a city champion or leader forms a committee and partners with a local organization that has affiliations with the proposed city (or country). The leader then presents the reasons for selecting a new sister city to the board of directors for consensus.

A Sarasota City Director (CD) and Assistant City Director (ACD) are then selected to lead the sister program and work with the counterpart international CD. The local CD is primarily responsible for initiating and setting up exchanges with the twinned sister city. A committee is formed of numerous other board members as well as other members of the association to plan and facilitate the exchanges.

Once a new sister city is selected a process of several years follows with the city first designated as a "Friendship City" that precedes formal signing by the respective mayors of the cities for selection as a full member "Sister City." The following are our friendship and sister cities listed in order of establishment as a twinned partner. Exchanges and activities with the sister cities are described in a subsequent chapter. The previous city directors are listed in chronology order at the end of each of the city descriptions. Emeritus status indicates that the city is no longer active as a sister city.

Santo Domingo (1963) (emeritus)
Hamilton, Canada (1990) (emeritus)
Perpignan, France (1994)
Vladimir, Russia (1994)
Tel Mond, Israel (1999)
Dunfermline, Scotland (2002)
Treviso, Italy (2007) (emeritus)
Siming District, Xiamen, China (2007)
Merida, Mexico (2010)
Raperswil-Jona, Switzerland, Friendship City (2014) (emeritus)
Busetto, Italy, Friendship City (2019)

Santo Domingo, Dominican Republic (1963)
Our First Sister City, Emeritus

Santo Domingo is the capital of the Dominican Republic and one of the oldest cities in the Caribbean. It is the cultural, commercial and political center of the Dominican Republic and the major seaport. The historical core of the city, the Zona Colonia, has numerous buildings from the 1500s including the ancient cathedral, the Alcázar de Colón castle and the Museo de las Casas Reales. There are numerous museums and eighteen universities in Santo Domingo with the Universidad Autónoma de Santo Domingo the oldest university in the Americas. The performing arts are ubiquitous with orchestra, opera, ballet, folkloric and musical concerts held in historic national venues.

Parque Colón in Santo Domingo (Photo R. Diesterheft)

Dallas Dort founded the first chapter of Sarasota Sister Cities by twinning with Santo Domingo in 1963, after a robust relationship had already been developed. Unfortunately, a military coup in late 1963 installed a junta that was eventually overthrown, but the relationship continued until emeritus status was established in 1990.

Street scene in Santo Domingo

Hamilton, Ontario, Canada (1990) Emeritus

Hamilton is a port city at the west end of Lake Ontario. Hamilton boasts a diversity of opportunities including educational, cultural and sightseeing attractions along with vibrant businesses and commerce. The city has a robust arts and culture community of art galleries, recording studios and the Hamilton Conservatory that hosts young actors, dancers, musicians, singers and visual artists. Significant programs are offered at the Professional Theatre Aquarius, the Royal Botanical Gardens, the Nautical Institute and the Art Gallery of Hamilton. McMasters University is the major institution of higher learning.

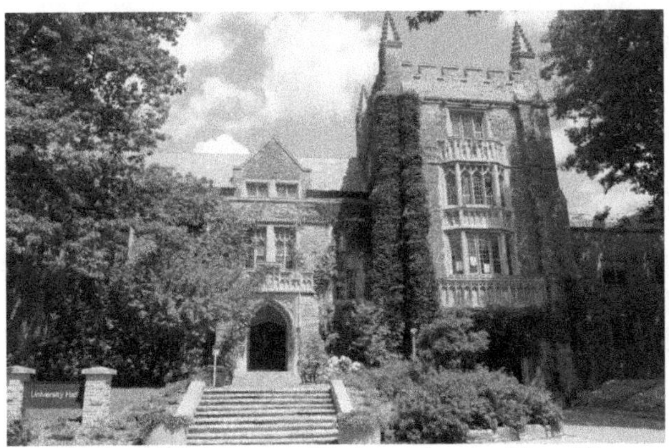

Hall at McMaster University in Hamilton

In 1990 Sarasota twinned with Hamilton, Ontario, Canada to build good will with our neighbors to the North. Hamilton Mayor Bob Morrow was instrumental in initiating the twinning and there were numerous exchanges until emeritus status was established. Previous City Directors are shown and listed below.

City Director Carol Furlong

Gloria Grenier (on right) served as City Director and Terry Neuss as Assistant City Director before the city went to emeritus status

Previous City Directors – Louis Maltaghati, Carole LaCentra, Carol Furlong, Gloria Grenier; Previous Assistant City Directors – Terry Neuss

Perpignan, France (1994)
The Genesis of the Sarasota Film Festival

Perpignan is situated on the Mediterranean coast of France and straddles the Catalan border of Spain. Catalan influence is dominant in the culture and cuisine. It is a convention city, university town and business center. Like Sarasota, it is a cultural mecca and features numerous monuments, churches and manors. Perpignan has long been a flourishing market center for wines, fruit and vegetables and most of the production is from the rich plain of the Languedoc-Roussillon region in which the city is located.

Perpignan train station is located at end of the Basse canal of the Tĕt river

The walled city is the site of the ancient Perpignan Cathedral, the 13th century Palace of the Kings of Majorca, the lavishly decorated Hôtel Pams Mansion and the Castillet fortress. A new National Theatre Archipelago was constructed in the 2011 to accommodate the growing performance arts culture in the city. The city hosts several important festivals including the Guitares au Palais music festival and the Visa pour I'Image festival of photojournalism. The University of Perpignan is one of the oldest in the region established in 1349 by King Peter IV of Aragon.

Historic Center of Perpignan

Sarasota twinned with Perpignan in 1994 with Sarasota Mayor Nora Patterson and the Mayor of Perpignan officially signing the partnership in Sarasota. This was followed by an official signing in Perpignan on September 7, 1995 by Perpignan Mayor Jean-Paul Alduy and Sarasota Mayor David Merrill.

Perpignan Mayor Jean-Paul Alduy and Sarasota Mayor Nora Patterson signing
Sister City Agreement in 1994
SCAS President Hope Byrnes is watching over standing on the right of picture

Oil Painting of Castillet on Basse
canal (Tĕt river) in Perpignan
by Ray Young in the SCAS office

Perpignan Castillet

SCAS delegation visit to Perpignan

Barbara Hopton (L) worked hard to bring Perpignan on as a Sister City and Barbara
Frey (R) served as a liaison with the Alliance Francaise de Sarasota

Alliance Member: Alliance Francaise de Sarasota
Previous City Directors – Alain Taulere, Myrna Welch, Barbara Hopton, Thierry
Chambon, Harry Dunn, Gloria Grenier, Marie de Neiges Grossas, currently Ivonne
A. Henry; Previous Assistant City Directors - Eva Frank, Emil Langlois

Perpignan CDs for many years (l to r)
Marie de Neiges Grossas,
Harry Dunn (w/ wife Happy) and Gloria Grenier

Emile Langlois served many years
as Assistant CD (w/ wife Pamela)

Vladimir, Russia (1994) - Rotary Ties

The City of Vladimir is renowned as the first capital of ancient Russia (Rus'), and is a part of the Golden Ring of ancient cities with rich culture and history. It is located on the east bank of the Klyazma River 114 miles northeast of Moscow.

Golden Ring of Russia

Golden Gate of Vladimir

Vladimir is in the Golden Ring of Russia with Moscow and other cities as shown in the graphic above. The city of Vladimir dates back to the 1100s with today's focus on development of tourism, the arts and education as well as industry. Two Russian Orthodox cathedrals in the city, the Cathedral of St. Demetrius and the Dormition Cathedral, were designated as part of a UNESCO World Heritage Site. Another impressive site in the city is the Golden Gate, which was originally a tower over the city's main gate built in 1195. There are numerous institutes of higher learning in Vladimir, notably Vladimir State University.

Sarasota twinned with Vladimir through a connection of the Rotary Club of the Keys in Sarasota which acted as a sponsor to a then-new club in Vladimir, one that continues today. On October 29, 1994, Sarasota Mayor Nora Patterson led a delegation to Vladimir for the first official signing of the partnership agreement. In April, 1995, a year that marked the Millennium Anniversary of the City of Vladimir, Mayor Igor Shimov led a large delegation for the official signing in Sarasota.

Dormition Cathedral in Vladimir

Signing of Vladimir as Sister City in 1994. Bottom row (l to r) Mayor Elena Potapova, Mayor Davie Merrill and SCAS President Hope Byrnes. Back row Vladimir delegation in Sarasota.

Laura Flesch was an intensely devoted CD in early years

Yulia Gaukhman

Olga Pliner

Miriam Jacobs

More Recent City Directors

Previous City Directors – Erika Cummings, Laura Flesch, Tatiana Baumshtyen, Larissa Trexler, Gundula Coleman, Yuliya Gaukhman, Olga Pliner, currently Miriam Kramer

Previous Assistant City Directors – Steven Briggs, Yelena Bychkovskikh, Boris Tsatskin, Nakolay Safonov, Albina Perets, Nancy Tsekou

Tel Mond Israel (1999)
A Jewish Federation/Betty Schoenbaum Initiative

The small city of Tel Mond was established in 1929 by Alfred Mond who purchased a citrus orchard in the Sharon Valley in which the city now stands. Tel Mond is located on the Mediterranean coast midway between Tel Aviv and Haifa. It has grown into one of the most livable cities in Israel. Tel Mond is a thriving regional center with an emphasis on arts, culture and education. The area boasts of excellent schools and programs in ballet, art, drama and gymnastics. The city supports a range of cultural interests and has a considerable senior citizen population.

Statue of Alfred Tel Mond

In 1999 Tel Mond became a new Sarasota Sister City. Mayor Shlomo Ratzabi and Sarasota Mayor Molly Cardamone signed the agreement in Sarasota while Sarasota Mayor Gene Pillot and Mayor Shlomo Ratzabi later conducted the official signing in Tel Mond. Many more interested people in Sarasota jumped on board, including philanthropist Betty Schoenbaum, who donated a library to Tel Mond.

Mayor Mollie Cardamone signs Sister City agreement
with Tel Mond Mayor in Sarasota

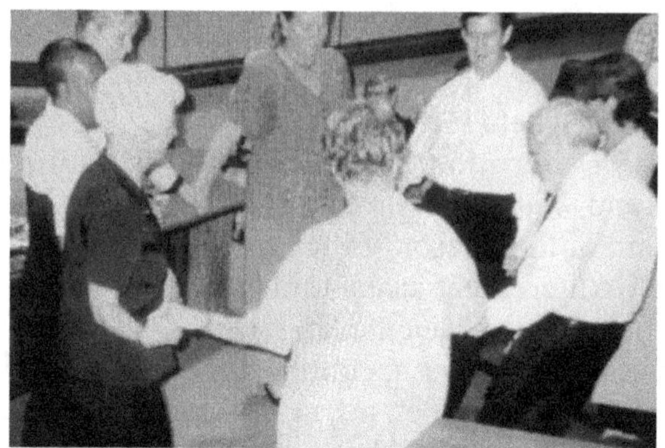

City mayor and commissioners dancing "Hora" after the signing of the Sister City Agreement with Tel Mond

Signing ceremony in Tel Mond

Tel Mond Mayor Shlomo Ratzabi (r) & Sarasota Mayor Gene Pillot (l)

Sarasota Mayor Gene Pillot (l) & former President of Israel Ehud Olmert

Below are four women who have devoted many hours to SCAS and Tel Mond programs as City Directors and Assistant City Directors

Linda Rosenbluth   Kim Sheintal   Alice Cotman   Betty Greenspan

Dr. Fred Bloom has assisted with many SCAS programs over the years and became the City Director for Tel Mond in 2023.

Tel Mond Alliance Member – Jewish Federation of Sarasota
Previous City Directors – Alice Cotman, Linda Rosenbluth, Betty Greenspan,
Marlies Gluck, Sidney Krupkin, Rabbi Jonathan Katz, Fred Bloom
Previous Assistant City Directors – Betty Greenspan, Alice Cotman, Kim Sheintal

Dunfermline, Scotland - (2002) Our Centennial Sister City
Dunfermline is the ancient capital of Scotland and is located just across the bridge
from Edinburgh in Fife. Not far away is the world-famous home of the St. Andrews
golf course. The city is the final resting place of King Robert the Bruce as well as
the birthplace of the famous philanthropist Andrew Carnegie. The city retains
much of its historical significance.

Notable features of the city are the ornate French Gothic style City Chambers, the
elegant spire atop the Old Sheriff Court and the Dunfermline Abbey, one of the best
examples of Scoto-Norman monastic architecture. The Dunfermline Carnegie
Library & Galleries provide the town with a museum, art gallery, archive, library,
café and gardens. The Alhambra serves as both a theatre and a live music venue.
Fife College is the major institution of higher learning in Dunfermline.

Dunfermline Abbey

The twinning was based on Sarasota being founded by Scots and the historical
significance of John Gillespie, a Scot, being the first mayor of Sarasota. He plotted
the city and built the first golf course in Sarasota. Another significant link between
the cities is that the Dunfermline Opera house was purchased and shipped to
Sarasota where it was reconstructed and refurbished as the current Merck Theater.
It is also known as the Asolo Repertory Theater and is adjacent to the Ringling
Museum and Mansion in Sarasota. The turn-of-the-century Dunfermline Opera
House had fallen into serious disrepair and restoration was not financially viable for
the community of Dunfermline.

Opera House in disrepair in Dunfermline   Restored as Merck Theater in Sarasota

In 2002, Dunfermline became Sarasota's Sister City during ceremonies at the Van Wezel Performing Arts Center followed by signing in the Dunfermline City Chamber. Also in 2002, a framed, full-size rubbing of Robert the Bruce was donated to the Asolo Theater and can be seen there today.

Signing of twinning agreement in Dunfermline (l to r),
seated - Sarasota City Commissioner Mary Quillin and Dunfermline Convener Tom Dair; standing – Mrs Tom Dair, Don Osborne, Dunfermline Co-Chair Gerry McMullan, SCAS President Linda Rosenbluth, SCAS City Director Bill Wallace, Dunfermline Co-Chair Keith Mason, Fife Area Law & Admin. Mgr. King Charles and Fife Councilor Alan Kenney

Bill Wallace   Susan Moir   Pauline Mitchell
Three devoted Dunfermline City Directors

Dunfermline Alliance Member – Caledonian Club of Sarasota
Previous City Directors – Don Osborne, Bill Wallace, Susan Moir, Gerard (Jerry) Kelly, currently Pauline Mitchell
Previous Assistant City Directors – Don Osborne, Ryan Clarke, Wallace Erickson, Mary Jo Heider, Karen Malesky

Treviso Province, Italy (2007) - Emeritus

Treviso Province, in the Veneto region of Italy, is located between Venice, the Adriatic and the foothills of the Italian Alps. In addition to the rich art and history treasures, the province of Treviso is one of Europe's most dynamic economic growth regions. The city of Treviso is laced with many canals and historic architecture. The Duomo features a neoclassical façade, a Romanesque crypt and a painting of Titian. The Palazzo del Trecento features vaulted arcades and the 16th century Fontana delle Tete fountain that was used to dispense wine.

A significant tie between the Province and Sarasota is that the Historic Asolo Theater in Sarasota was originally the Opera House of Queen Cornaro in the town of Asolo, Italy. It was purchased, crated and shipped to Sarasota where it was reconstructed for modern performances on the grounds of the Ringling Museum.

Mayor Fredd Atkins, (l to r), Treviso Mayor Leonardo Muraro and SCAS City Director Mirco Chiodi signing Sister City Agreement in the Historic Asolo Theater in 2007

It was on the stage of the Historic Asolo Theater in Sarasota where the partnership was signed between Mayor Fredd Atkins and the President of Treviso Province Leonardo Muraro on February 29, 2007. The twinning resulted in a rich, active exchange program aided by the interest of alliance organizations such as the Ausonia Society and the Italian Club of Sarasota.

Historic Asolo Theater after move from Asolo, Itlay and reconstruction at the site of the Ringling Musuem in Sarasota.

Micro Chiodi   Susanna Wriston & Alexandra DeStefanis   Anna Madaschi
Micro was the first CD followed by Susanna, Alexandra and Anna

Previous City Directors - Mirco Chiodi, Alexandra DeStefanis, Anna Madaschi, Susanna Wriston
Previous Assistant City Directors - Bruno Pasquale, Joe Loccisano, Fredrica Priano, Susanna Wriston, Isabelle Eidet

Xiamen Siming District, Fujian Province, China (2007)

Xiamen is located in the Fujian Province of Southern China just across the China Sea from Taiwan. It was ranked as China's second "most suitable city for living" in 2006, as well as China's "most romantic leisure city" in 2011. Xiamen is a convention city with an annual international trade fair, a sports center for golf, water-sports and martial arts and holds the Xiamen International Marathon each March. It has a wealth of cultural and educational resources such as the prestigious Xiamen University, public art displays, symphony orchestras, opera companies, jazz group. It also is a center for health care, sports medicine and complementary medicine.

There are numerous high level programs for improvement of agriculture, aquaculture, horticulture, and marine biology in Xiamen. The city has a major international airport and a seaport designated as a Special Economic Zone for foreign trade. The Siming District, in the historic old town of Xiamen, is on the sheltered Yundang Bay. A special Educational and Cultural Center is located in the district as well as one of the largest piano museums in the world.

China has such large cities that it was difficult to find a pairing that was right for Sarasota. The Siming District of Xiamen was recognized as a good fit as a sister city by Ringling College of Art professor Dr. Carolyn Bloomer, a frequent visitor to China. The District comprises only five percent of the city but has a population of one million people.

In 2007, Xiamen (Siming District) became twinned with Sarasota. An enthusiastic Sarasota delegation led by Mayor Lou Ann Palmer participated in the signing ceremonies in Xiamen during June 5-11, 2007. The Sarasota signing was conducted by Mayor Palmer at a public ceremony on October 9, 2007 in the old Federal Building in downtown Sarasota. Several Chinese-American Associations also participated in this pairing.

Signing celebration of Sister City Agreement in Xiamen by Mayor Lou Ann Palmer accompanied by SCAS delegation of Xiamen City Director Carolyn Bloomer, Tel Mond City Director Linda Rosenbluth and VP-Education Ray Young

Gift presented to Mayor Lou Ann Palmer by the Siming District Official at the signing ceremony, now displayed in our Sister City Office in the Federal Bldg, Sarasota.

Carolyn Bloomer   Douglas Sparks   Kun Shi

Former City Directors   Current City Director

Xiamen Alliance Member – Southwest Florida Chinese Association
Previous City Directors - Carolyn Bloomer, Douglas Sparks, currently Kun Shi
Previous Assistant City Directors - Ed Lin, Quinhong Wei, Irene Leung, Hongying
Liu, Li Volk, and currently Larry Bennison, Duane Finger and Douglas Sparks

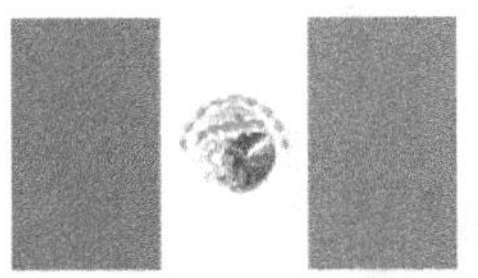

Merida, Yucatan, Mexico (2010)

Located 180 miles west of Cancun in the Yucatán Peninsula, Merida has many
similarities to Sarasota such as location near the Gulf of Mexico, a tropical type
climate, being a regional center of higher education and sharing a love for culture
and the arts. The city has several universities including the Autonomous University
of the Yucatan as well as the Yucatan Symphony Orchestra featuring classical
music, jazz and opera.

This colonial city has one of the largest historical centers in the Americas with
many of the Spanish colonial buildings from its wealthy past remaining.
It is also an ideal spot from which to explore Mayan culture and important Mayan
archeological sites like Chechen Itza and Uxmal. The city Mérida is one of eight
safe and popular marquee tourist spots that are exempt from U.S. State Department
cautions against non-essential travel in Mexico.

On December 19, 2010, Mérida, Yucatán, México was twinned with Sarasota.
Mayors Angélica Araujo Lara of Mérida and Kelly Kirschner of Sarasota signed the
official twinning documents on a beautiful Florida day in the Courtyard of the John
and Mabel Ringling Museum of Art. Student musicians from the Sarasota Military
Academy performed at the ceremony.

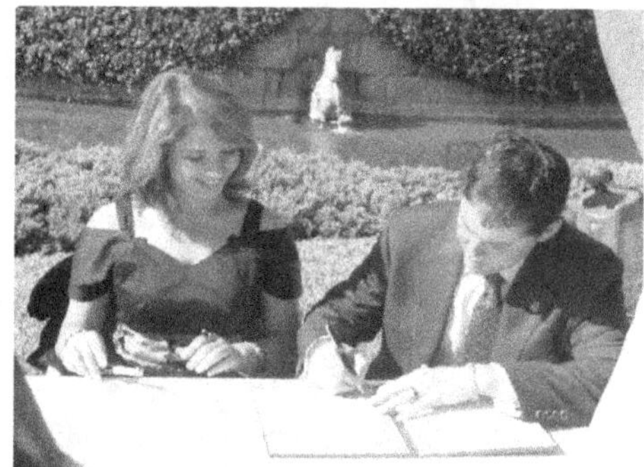

The signing ceremony between Merida and Sarasota took place at the Ringling Museum by Mayors Angélica Araujo Lara of Mérida and Kelly Kirschner of Sarasota with the entrance progression led by bagpipers from the Sarasota Military Academy

Grisell Aleman and Mike Fehily have served as both City Directors and Assistant City Directors for Merida for many years
Previous City Directors - Javier Curiel, Michael Fehily, currently Grisell Aleman
Previous Assistant City Directors - Gipsian Salazar, Eleanor Williams

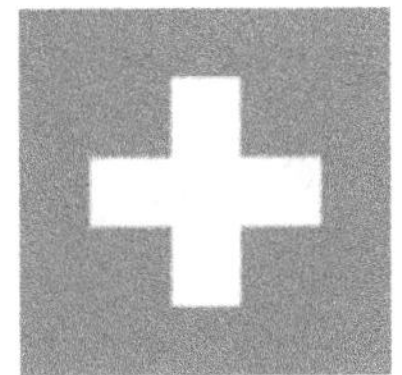

Rapperswil-Jona, Switzerland Friendship City (2014)
Emeritus

Rapperswil-Jona is located in the Canton St. Gallen on the upper end of Lake Zurich and is known as the City of Roses. This medieval city boasts beautiful scenic vistas, a rich cultural life, extensive hiking trails and water sports in a Mediterranean holiday atmosphere. The medieval center of the city is a vehicle-free with sites of the Polish Museum and the Knies Children's Zoo. There is a nearby picturesque lake resort and a classic historic wooden bridge to Hurden.

The 100 year old circus company, Circus Knie, was founded in Rapperswil-Jona and the long history mirrors that of the circus focus in Sarasota, the former home of the Ringling and Barnum Circus. Rapperswil-Jona and Sarasota became Friendship cities in 2014. A Friendship City is a prelude to a Sister City. This effort was supported by the Swiss American Club of Sarasota.

Signing of Rapperswil-Jona by Sarasota Mayor Willie Shaw and looking on are R-J City Director Nelly Camardo, SCAS President Beth Ruyle and Primo Bader

Harbor in Rapperswil and in the background Rapperswil Castle
and St. John's Church

City Director - Nelly Camardo

Assistant City Director - Charlotte Hull

Busseto, Italy Friendship City (2019)

Busseto is located in the province of Parma, in Emila-Romagna of northern Italy. The town and many of the sites are linked to the famous Maestro Giuseppe Verdi. The nearby village of Le Roncole was the site of Verdi's birth in 1813 and near the main square is Cas Barezzi, the headquarters of the Friends of Verdi. There are also several churches where Verdi played the organ and the Palazzo Orlandi, an ornate house, where Verdi completed several of his compositions. He lived in Villa Verdi from 1848 to the end of his life in 1901. Additional highlights include the Teatro Giuseppe Verdi and the National Museum of Guiseppe Verdi.

Busseto is our newest Friendship City and is in the process of completing a Sister Cities relationship. Phillip Gordon worked with Sarasota Maestro Victor DiRenzi to have Busseto in line to be our next sister city.

City Director Philip Gordon was "instrumental" in establishing our ties to Busseto.

Alliance Member - Italian Club of Sarasota
Previous City Director - Philip Gordon, currently Jeanne Murphy
Previous Assistant City Director - Kenney DeCamp, currently Dennis Ciborowski

SCAS Board of Directors

SCAS is led by a Board of Directors elected by the overall membership. There are currently 22 officers with a quorum of 12 members. A sample of the organizational structure is shown in the figure below. The functions and duties of the board members are described in following chapters and the names and short bios of some recent members are provided at the end of the book to illustrate the range of expertise on the board. We have a Sarasota city director and one or more assistant city directors for each of our Sister Cities and Friendship Cities. There is a vice president for each of our functional areas, and a treasurer, a secretary and a youth ambassador.

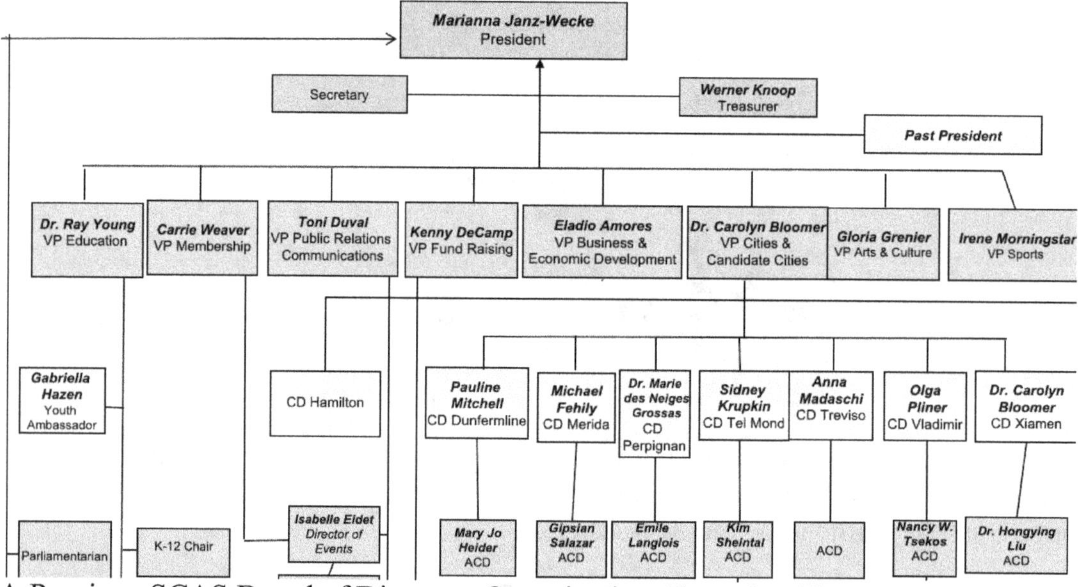

A Previous SCAS Board of Directors Organization Chart that illustrates the designated positions on the Board.

Each member of the Executive Committee of the Board of Directors reports to the Board. Board members serve as an Officer of the Corporation in accordance with State of Florida incorporation requirements. Under Article VI, Section 1 of the By-laws, each officer is elected by the Board of Directors at the annual meeting and holds office year to year. Our Board usually meets once a month. The meetings are chaired by the President and were conducted on Zoom during the pandemic.

Past Presidents

Founding members of SCAS (l to r)
Dr. John Elmendorf, **First President Dallas Dort** and Dr. George Baughman
Dallas Dort 1963-1967

Donald Spivey 1968-1975   Wells Purmort 1976-1986   Julio Claret 1989-1991

Asim Mohammed 1992-1994 (not pictured)

Hope Byrnes
1994-2001

Linda Rosenbluth
2001-2005

William Wallace
2005-2008

Carla Rayman
2008-2011

Tom Halbert
2011-2013

Beth Ruyle Hullinger
2013-2016, 2018-2019

Mariana Janz-Wecke
2016-218

Toni Duval
2019-2021

Miriam Kramer
2021-2023

Diana Forman-Friedman
2023

Sarasota City Hall on First Street
SCAS is partially supported by the City of Sarasota and works in coordination with city officials for exchanges with our sister cities.

Functions and Duties of SCAS Board Members

Following are general descriptions of the functions and duties of the SCAS Board Members. Included are some of the significant events that the board members have facilitated for SCAS. All the previous holders of the board title are listed at the end of each description. A further detailed listing of all the duties of each office is provided near the end of the book.

Board of Directors in 2017 (l to r), Nelly Camardo, Kenney DeCamp, Ray Young, Carrie Weaver, Carolyn Bloomer, Anna Madaschi, Gloria Grenier, Werner Knoop, Pauline Mitchell, Toni Duval and President Marianna Janz-Wecke

Zoom Board of Directors meeting in days of Covid

City Directors

The City Directors (CDs) are responsible for maintaining contacts with their counter-part in their sister city and for initiating all exchanges and events with the sister city. The many exchanges and events that the CDs have arranged and completed are described in the section on Exchange Programs and Activities.

Vice Presidents

The Vice Presidents perform specific functions as described below and assist the City Directors in all the exchange programs. The Vice Presidents also oversee and assist with programs that encompass more than one sister city. All the previous Vice Presidents are listed for each of the VP positions.

Vice President - Arts and Culture

Tel Mond Dancers

Sarasota Sister Cities is very active in promoting arts and culture within Sarasota and our sister cities. The VP-Arts and Culture works closely with the City Directors to arrange many exchanges of real and digital art and photography as well as exchanges of artists between our sister cities. One of our most significant programs that is held annually in conjunction with the Florida Studio Theatre (FSU) is the "Write a Play Competition and Young Playwrights Festival." Entries of short plays composed by young playwrights are received from students in our sister cities and winning entries are invited to Sarasota to see their plays performed on stage by professional actors from FST. This joint sister city program is further described in the section below on Joint Exchange Programs.

Former VP-Arts & Culture
Gloria Grenier was also our SCAS Treasurer

Sue Gordon

Previous VP of Art and Culture: Jerry Roucher, Hope Byrnes, Carolyn Bloomer, Liliane Sealy-Schrock, Jane Rose, Ron Gossett, Gloria Grenier, Susan Gordon, Wendy Lerner (current)

Vice President - Cities and Candidate Cities

The Vice President of Cities and Candidate cities leads the City Directors of our Sister Cities and Friendship Cities. The VP conducts meetings with the city directors and ensures that new City Directors (CD) learn their role. Monthly meetings of the City Directors are coordinated and led by the VP of Cities to discuss future exchanges, handle any difficulties with their programs and assure that there is no overlap of exchanges to and from Sarasota.

A recent VP-Cities & Candidate Cities Rabbi Jonathan Katz, also served as City Director of Tel Mond

Beth-Ruyle Hullinger former VP-Cities & Candidate Cities and SCAS President

Previous VP of Cities and Candidate Cities – David Laws, Carol Furlong, Mirco Chiodi, Harry Dunn, Linda Rosenbluth, David Harralson, Carolyn Bloomer, Beth Ruyle-Hullinger, Miriam Kramer, Rabbi Jonathan Katz, Pauline Mitchell (current)

Vice President – Communication

The communication team developed our SCAS website a number of years ago and it is regularly updated at sarasotasistercities.org. A database of our members (iMembers) is maintained for regular communication with our members as well as for all those who have shown interest or have a need to know about our organization. Regular e-mail messages are sent about SCAS activities and other significant community events.

An informative SCAS Newsletter is published frequently that covers impending events, activities and lectures. The newsletter also includes coverage by the VP-Communication of recent exchanges with our sister cities, information from Sister Cities International and stories and descriptions about exchanges by other sister city organizations. Recent newsletters are provided on our sister city website (sarasotasistercities.org)

A further description of SCAS activities and events is provided in an array of different social media websites that include many pictures of our members and supporters. They can be viewed at https://photossarasotasistercities.blogspot.com. You can view older editions of our Newsletter on our website sarasotasistercities.org and bridgestotheworldssc.blogspot.com. The output of our strategy session can be reviewed at sscplan.blogspot.com. A number of these sites are also listed in the last section of the book on "Links and References."

Craig Hullinger created many additional social media sites for SCAS
Craig served as VP-Communication and also VP-Economic Development for many years

Toni Duval   Jana Stanley
Two more recent VP-Communication

Previous VP of Communication – Barbara Bartz, Bill Mallett, Bill Sikes, John "Tom" Halbert, Jan Thomas, Toni Duval, Craig Hullinger, Jana Stanley, Ayanna Coleman (current)
Marketing and Strategic Communications Intern – Wynona Dean (USF)
Previous Publicity Directors – Tom Halbert, Wallace Erickson, David Lionel

Vice President - Economic Development

The Vision
To provide quality jobs at good wages while improving the environment in our community.

Mission Statement
We are committed to providing an environment in which our natural resources, our people, and our economy are balanced. We will not compromise the future by focusing solely on the needs of today. We aspire to have our regional community leaders develop, promote, and improve the quality of our community through sustainable practices.

Sustainable Economic Development
Sustainable "Green" Economic Development combines environmental improvement and traditional economic development into one discipline. Traditional economic development can be employed to increase employment while improving our environment. Economic Development and "Green" Development can be synergistic, improving our overall quality of life.

Sarasota Sister Cities has developed programs to help facilitate the sustainable economic development of our Region and of our Sister Cities. Sarasota is a great place to start or expand your business and our Sister Cities Association is ready to help you expand your business into their countries.

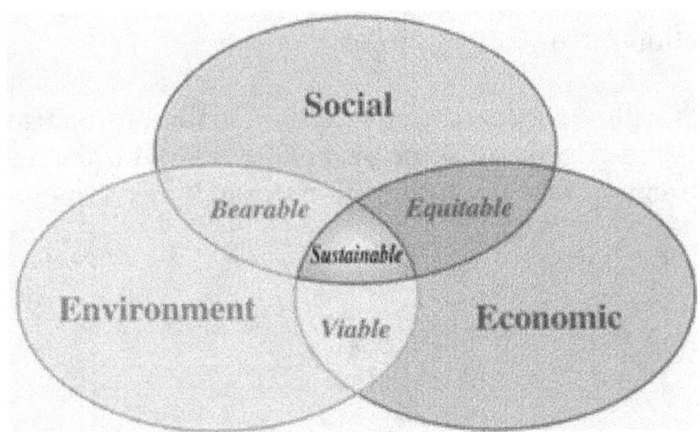

Our Blog for Sustainable Economic Development is: sarasotasistercities.com that forwards to sarasotasistercities.blogspot.com.
An economic development brochure has also been produced for dissemination and is included in the Brochures section of this book. Our strategy is summarized in four points: 1. Keep our businesses and jobs, 2. Expand the businesses we have, 3. Enhance our community for business, 4. Protect and improve our environment

Proposals to improve our City and Its Environs
We have developed several proposals for strategic sustainable improvement of our community as described in the blogs below. We periodically propose these possible improvements to the government and the private sector in the community: giftsforsarasota.blogspot.com, sarasotatownsquare.blogspot.com, Honorepark.blogspot.com.

Additional websites, links and references are provided in the end section of the book.
Previous VP of Economic Development – John Brown, Carla Rayman, John Freeman, Anthony Homer, Charles Steilen, Kenney DeCamp, Eladio Amores, currently Craig Hullinger

Vice President – Fundraising

Sarasota Sister Cities is financed by membership dues, charitable contributions, support from the City of Sarasota, and regular fund raising events. Raising money is an important function for any organization.

SCAS participates with the local Community Foundation of Sarasota County (CFSC) in fundraising efforts. In some years CFSC provides matching gifts that provide valuable funding for our organization through the "Giving Challenge" program.

Funding is improved if donors are informed of the use of the funds. Our theme in 2018 was funding for training teachers from our sister cities on how to educate and help students to write plays for submission to the "Young Playwrights Competition" held at the Florida Studio Theater, as described above in the VP-Arts and Culture section. The effort raised $8,000 for the exchange and training. Three teachers were chosen for the training session from Perpignan, Treviso and Tel Mond.

We also raised substantial funds by conducting a Telethon in the Media room of City Hall that was covered by our local SNN TV station. This giving partner effort raised $14,682 from donations and the matching funds. Special thanks were afforded to Finance Co-Chairman Bill Wallace and Kenney DeCamp as well as Gloria Grenier, Carolyn Bloomer, David Harralson, and Craig Hullinger who worked the phones at the Telethon, and Bill Mallet who set up the equipment.

Bill Wallace worked tirelessly for many years raising considerable amounts of funding for SCAS

Previous VP of Fundraising – Dennis Wonn, Bill Wallace, Kenney DeCamp, Betty Greenspan, Karen Lyon

Vice President - Membership

Membership is vital to any organization. The recruitment and retention of qualified members is key to the success of Sarasota Sister Cities. The VP of Membership works hard to attract and retain members. Working with the VP of Events and the VP of Communication, he or she ensures that our new members are engaged and involved. The website, contact database, emails and attendance at events are vital to maintain membership in the organization.

David Harralson Isabelle Eidet
Recent VP-Membership

Previous VP of Membership – Kamala Long, Carla Rayman, Bill Mallett, David Harralson, Drew Deininger, John "Tom" Halbert, David Harralson, Mike Adkinson, Carrie Weaver, Mary Ellen McMahon, Isabelle Eidet.

Vice President - Education

The function of the VP-Education is to create and maintain links with educational institutions in both Sarasota and our sister cities with the goal of involving students at all levels (elementary, high school and college) in our programs and exchanges. The "Write a Play Competition and Young Playwrights Festival" held in conjunction with the Florida Studio Theater, as described above in the VP-Arts and Culture section, is a good example of our involvement of students from many of our sister cities in our SCAS program in Sarasota. The students are invited to Sarasota for about a week and are further exposed to other cultural and educational amenities in Sarasota. They engage in local activities, sightseeing and meeting government officials.

There is also a student representative on our SCAS Board of Directors that serves as a student ambassador. The VP-Education is responsible for enlisting a student from the Girls and Boys Club of Sarasota, introducing the student to the Board and mentoring the progress of the student. The student serves to greet visiting exchange students and serves as a direct liaison with students from our sister cities. Several previous student ambassadors set up an SCAS student Facebook page for student interaction.

Previous Youth Ambassadors - Kimberly Modic, Vince Giura, Ian Krouse, Max Martinez, Ray Odeh, Taylor Press, Stephanie Martinez, Chela Bell, Morgan Bortz, Gabriella Hazan, Anni Abassy, Suné Venter, Abigail Sweitzer, Wynona Dean

 Roberta Somach   Former VPs    Dawn Graber

Former VP-Education Ray Young on left with SCAS Board members and Teachers from our Sister Cities visiting Ringling College of Art & Design; (l to r) Ray Young, Perpignan teacher Hadda LaMotte, Ringling College representative, SCAS CD-Treviso Susanna Wriston, Treviso teacher Elisa Carollo, Tel Mond teacher Idit Levy, SCAS President Marianna Janz-Wecke and SCAS VP-Arts & Culture Gloria Grenier.

VP-Education Ray Young produced a five part series of You-Tube presentation videos that describe our SCAS organization and our Sister Cities as listed below with the URL. Videos online at https//videossarasotasistercities.blogspot.com
SCAS Part I – <u>Selection of Sister Cities and Administration</u>
    https://youtu.be/qt5k3X2Gx1Y?si=mOgzlWPy4wTFIULi
SCAS Part II – <u>Innovation Awards & Sister Cities Perpignan & Tel Mond</u>
    https://youtu.be/4_M8jEoMlLY?si=ruXRGJKoO5CJc0Dp
SCAS Part III – <u>Sister Cities Dunfermline & Xiamen</u>
    https://youtu.be/1qblQd5ttmg?si=w-AEbpeeNpZVD3Fi
SCAS Part IV – <u>Sister Cities Treviso, Merida, Vladimir & Rapperswil-Jona</u>
    https://youtu.be/lOeXFKCgOF0?si=WD5xxF8qWfqCEb33
SCAS Part V – <u>Community Activities of SCAS</u>
    https://youtu.be/18QNESBvdhs?si=8Xjmi0ti-MX-GOhQ

Previous VP of Education – Roberta Somach, Liliane Sealy-Schrock, Carolyn Bloomer, Raymond Young, Dawn Graber, Ellie Stoll
Previous High School Teacher Liaisons – Lydia McIntire, Bridget Coughlin

Vice President – Sports

Sister Cities supports a number of sporting exchanges and competitions with our Sister Cities. The VP-Sports is responsible for initiating exchanges in all areas of sports, especially those with facilities in Sarasota such as golf, rowing, baseball, basketball, tennis and pickleball. This VP works closely with the City Directors for coordination and facilitation of the exchanges and several sports exchanges have occurred in past years and described in the section below on exchanges.

SCAS members have assisted with the international Dragon Boat Races held annually at Benderson Park in Sarasota

SCAS assisted with the International Lawn Bowling Competition in Sarasota, 2016

Richard Greenspan was a recent VP-Sports

Previous VP of Sports – Scott Treibly, Joe LaRusso, Bill Wallace, Lawrence Lonson, Kenney DeCamp, Irene Leung, Richard Greenspan, E. Ramey (current)

VP-Programs and Planning

Sarasota Sister Cities provides a number of excellent programs for our members and the general Sarasota community. Our monthly luncheons include a featured speaker with topics ranging from sister city exchanges and programs to descriptions of organizations in our local community. For example, presidents or representatives of such institutions as Mote Marine Laboratories, Selby Gardens, New College, University of South Florida, Ringling Museum, Asolo Theater, Florida State Theater, etc. have provided luncheon presentations.

Another monthly event is held at the Selby Library and features presentations from community leaders and local government. Topics include new developments in the city, international travel and philanthropic activities. A listing of some of the mix of diverse presentations provided in the past is given in a subsequent section. The Selby Library presentations are followed by a Meet and Greet at a local restaurant.

The attractive Selby Library in downtown Sarasota

Ray Young was the first to hold the new position of VP-Programs & Planning and served in the position for ten years and five years as VP-Education

Previous VP of Programs & Planning – Raymond Young, Beth Ruyle, Julianne Bosch

Director of Events

The Events Planner works in coordination with the VP-Programs & Planning and VP-Membership. The person coordinates luncheons at Bird Key Yacht Club and at our large Annual Gala that also serves as a fundraiser.

Previous Events Planners – Jane Wood, Linda & Richard Frary, Gayle Maxey, Carrie Weaver, Isabelle Eidet, Gail Sanderson, Karen Malesky, Sylva Kanderal, Charlotte Hull, Linda Mercurio

Charlotte Hull and Isabelle Eidet have arranged and worked at many SCAS events including luncheons, the Annual Gala and Holiday Gatherings

Charlotte Hull and Sylvia Kanderal tended the registration desk for many SCAS luncheons at the Bird Key Yacht Club

Kenney DeCamp has played an integral role in arranging and setting up numerous SCAS events over the years. He has been the Master of Ceremonies for several Gala dinners and has served as VP-Fundraising, VP-Sports and Assistant Director for our sister city Busetto, Italy.

Gayle Maxey was involved with many SCAS events and initiated our first of many popular "Happy Hour, Meet & Greet" social gatherings. She also served as our SCAS secretary.

Treasurer

The Treasurer ensures that the organization is fiscally sound with excellent financial management. The program Quickbooks is used to provide clear and understandable financial statements. The organization raises and spends about $30,000 a year. In most years income and outgo are roughly balanced. An independent CPA annually conducts a thorough audit.

Sister Cities Association of Sarasota is financed by membership dues, charitable contributions, fundraising events and support from the City of Sarasota. Raising money is, of course, very important for any organization.

Funds are raised with registration and a silent auction at our One World Gala. We also have received funding from the Sarasota Community Foundation through a community wide fundraising appeals. Some of these Giving Challenges have been supported by the Patterson Foundation with occasional matching funds offered to non-profit organizations in the community.

For example, in 2015 our very successful Giving Partner effort was covered by the local TV station SNN. Donations to SCAS were $6,841 and with matching funds resulted in a total of $12,932. An additional $1,750 was also received after the campaign but not matched. Our total fundraising for that event came to $14,682. We are most appreciative of the financial support and to our volunteers for their great effort.

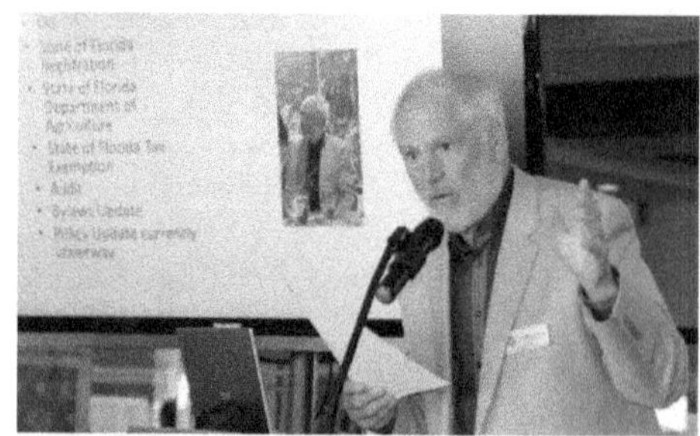

Treasurer Werner Knoop providing financial report at a SCAS luncheon

Recent Treasurer Gloria Grenier

Previous Treasurers – Carol Furlong, David Plaskett, Mary Ferrara, John Mitchell, Arif Shurdha, Jerry Ogle, David Praxisas, John Quartuccio, Werner Knoop, Gloria Grenier, Dennis Ciborowski (current)

City Hall Liaison

Bill Mallett was employed as a webmaster with the City of Sarasota and helped develop our first SCAS website. He also served as the VP-Communication for SCAS and a valuable liaison to the city for many years.

Prrevious City Hall Liaisons: Billy Robinson, Jim Freeman, Jason Lippa, Bill Mallett, Pamela Nadalini, Heather Essa, Robert Shanley

Historian

Judy Caldwell-Moore was our only SCAS historian and she accumulated many news articles, pictures and newsletters that made it possible to produce this book on our sixty year history. Past newsletters are available at: Bridgestotheworldssc.blogspot.com

Parliamentarian/Protocol

Liliane Sealy-Schrock served as the SCAS Parliamentarian for many years as well as President of the Sarasota Key Rotary Club
Previous Parliamentarian/Protocol: Howard Cowell, John Brown, Liliane Sealy-Schrock

Secretary

The secretary records the minutes of our monthly board meetings and assures distribution to the board members.

Previous SCAS Secretaries: Laura Clare, Helen Janssen, Betty Plaskett, John Tucillo, Carole LaCentra, Gabriela Kepecz, Grace McKee, Gundula Coleman, Lora Bedford, Beverly Ulrey, Jane Passman, Gloria Grenier, Beth Ruyle-Hullinger, Nelly Camardo, Virginia Stephens, Byron Hill, Sue Gordon,
Xochitl Napoles (current)

Newsletter

A SCAS newsletter is produced frequntly that provides updates on SCAS activites exchanges and programs. The newsletter is now produced by the VP-Communications but previously it was composed by a designated newsletter position formerly held by: Salie O'Malley, Jan Schneider, Jan Thomas

Keeping it real (l to r), VP-Communications Jana Stanley, Director of Events Isabelle Eidet, President Toni Duval, President Miriam Kramer.

Strategy Sessions

In addition to regular monthly meetings of SCAS board members there are also occasional strategy meeting held to assess our programs and chart the future based on the priorities expressed by the attendees. These sessions have been led by Beth Ruyle, Craig Hullinger and Toni Duval who all had previous professional experience and expertise in facilitating the sessions.

Strategy session for SCAS Board of Directors facilitated by President Toni Duval Standing (l to r) Beth Ruyle-Hullinger, Dawn Graber, Philip Gordon, Toni Duval, Miriam Kramer, Gloria Grenier and Ray Young. Seated is Pauline Mitchell.

The **output of a strategy** session can be reviewed at **sscplan.blogspot.com**

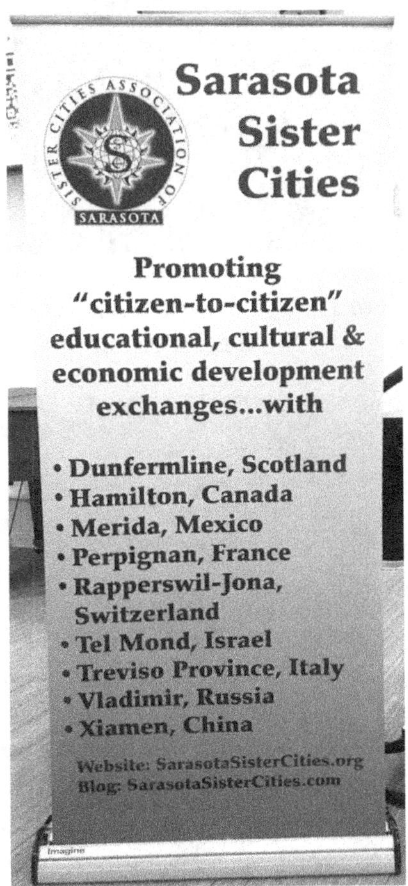

Banner displayed at our SCAS events

Relationship of SCAS with City Mayors and Commissioners

SCAS is partially supported by the City of Sarasota and works in coordination with city officials for exchanges with our sister cities. Frequently a city mayor or commissioner participates in an exchange program and especially for the official signing of the twinning agreement. During every exchange visit to Sarasota our mayors and city commissioners graciously greet our visiting delegations. At the welcoming session at City Hall gifts are exchanged and photographs are taken for publication in local outlets. It is a warm demonstration of citizen diplomacy at the individual level.

Sarasota Mayor and City Commissioners in 2023 (l to r)
Debbie Trice, Vice Mayor Liz Alpert, Eric Arroyo, Mayor Kyle Battie and
Jen Ahearn-Koch

Former Sarasota Mayors and Commissioners
(l to r) Mayor Fredd Atkins, Mayor Lou Ann Palmer, Mayor Willie Shaw,
Commissioner Susan Chapman, in back Mayor Kelly Kirschner

The following is a list of the mayors and city commissioners who have served during our sister city signings, exchanges and/or greetings over the years. SCAS is very grateful for their encouragement and strong support over the past 60 years.

Year	Mayor	Sister Cities
1963-1968	Hershel Hayo, David Cohen, Jack Betz	Santo Domingo
1968-1976	Jack Betz, D. William Overton, Gerald Ludwig, Fred Soto, Elmer Berkel, J. "Tony" Saprito	Santo Domingo
1976-1989	Ronald Norman, Elmer Berkel, Fred Soto, Rita Roehr, Annie Bishopric, Lou Ann Palmer, William Kline, Kerry Kirschner, Fredd Atkins	Santo Domingo
1989-1994	Lou Ann Palmer, Kerry Kirschner Fredd Atkins, Jack Gurney, Gene Pillot	Hamilton, Ontario
1994-2000	Nora Patterson, David Merrill, Mollie Cardamone, Gene Pillot, Jerome Dupree	Vladimir, Russia Perpignan, France Tel Mond, Israel
2000-2004	Gene Pillot, Albert Hogel, Carolyn Mason, Lou Ann Palmer	Dunfermline, Scotland
2005-2008	Richard Martin, Mary Ann Servian, Fredd Atkins, Lou Ann Palmer	Treviso, Italy Xiamen, China
2008-2012	Lou Ann Palmer, Richard Clapp, Kelly Kirschner, Susan Atwell	Merida, Mexico
2013-2018	Shannon Snyder, Willie Shaw, Shelli Freeland Eddie, Liz Alpert	Rapperswil-Jona
2018-2023	Liz Alpert, Jen Ahearn-Koch, Hagen Brody Erik J. Arroyo, Kyle Battie	Busseto, Italy

Appreciation is also expressed to City Manager Tom Barwin (l) and his successor Marlon Brown who have been very supportive of SCAS over the years

Former Sarasota Mayors
Front (l to r) Mollie Cardamone, Rita Roehr, Jerome Dupree, Fred Soto. Lou Ann Palmer; Back (l to r) Kelly Kirschner, David Merrill, Bill Kline, Elmer Berkel, and Richard Clapp

Annual presentation by SCAS President and supporting SCAS members to the Mayor and City Commissioners about the accomplishment of our organization. Continued funding is the decided and voted upon by the City Council at the session

Exchange Programs and Activities with Our Sister Cities

There has been an impressive number of activities and exchanges with our sister cities over the past sixty years. Artistic exchanges have involved artists, real and virtual art, and photography. There is also a display of art on the Bayfront of Sarasota with the Embracing Our Differences program further described in the section on Joint Projects. Student exchanges have involved school visits, dance, song, circus performance and science. Delegation exchanges have included city officials, Sister City officers and members and members of the community.

In this section some notable interactions are described although many more have occurred over the years. Some of the exchanges involved several of our sister cities and these are described in a separate section "Joint Sister City Projects and Exchanges" following the descriptions of the exchange programs for each of the sister cities provided below.

Santo Domingo (1963) (emeritus)

Santo Domingo was established as a sister city with the formation of SCAS in 1963. A military coup in late 1963 only temporarily delayed exchanges between the cities that included rotary clubs and student exchanges. Additional activities and exchanges were spurred when Wells Purmort, a long-term member, accepted the SCAS presidency in 1976. A street was then named for Sarasota, "Avenida Sarasota" in Santo Domingo, and similarly the "Plaza Santo Domingo" was established in Sarasota.

Plaza Santo Domingo near the Municipal Auditorium in Sarasota

---

During visits to Santo Domingo it was determined that the city was in need of a number of important materials, supplies and vehicles. Mayors Gene Pillot and Lou Ann Palmer visited Santo Domingo and arranged to have a Sarasota Fire Truck donated to the city. The truck was driven to Miami where is it was shipped to Santo Domingo. This was followed by the Sarasota Memorial Hospital donating medicine and medical equipment to Santo Domingo. After a devastating hurricane in Santo Domingo, the Sarasota School Board donated school desks, books and supplies to the city.

Students from Santo Domingo shown above visited Sarasota in 1964 after Riverview High School students visited Santo Domingo in 1963 (Sarasota H-T)

Later a Santo Domingo marine biologist became an intern at Mote Marine Laboratories in Sarasota. Additional exchanges during this period involved scout organizations, Rotary and Kiwanis Clubs and business people.

Hamilton, Canada (1990) (emeritus)

Mayor Fredd Atkins lead a delegation to Hamilton for the official signing ceremony. Included in the delegation was the Sarasota Ballet that performed in the Hamilton Theatre Aquarius. This was followed by a visit of the John Laing Singers from Hamilton who participated in the First United Methodist Fine Art Series in Sarasota.

Sarasota Mayor Richard Martin greeting Hamilton Mayor Richard Di Ianni, 2004

The John Laing Singers from Hamilton performed to a full house at the Church of the Redeemer in downtown Sarasota during the exchange visit.

An exchange of Gerontology students from McMaster University in Hamilton and University of South Florida took place between the cities. Elementary school art was also exchanged for a Sister Cities Children Art Show.

A unique exchange of News anchors Vida Urbonis of WWSB-TV Sarasota with Dan McClean of CHCH-TV Hamilton took place between the sister cities. This was followed by the 20th year anniversary of the Sister City relationship with Hamilton recognized by hosting volunteers from Hamilton's Westfield Heritage Village for a visit to Sarasota organized by CD Gloria Grenier.

News Anchors

Vita Urbonis
Sarasota

Dan McClean
Hamilton

Ontario Royal Botanical Garden in Hamilton

Perpignan, France (1994

Sarasota and Perpignan have hosted many activities over the years. A close relationship with the Alliance Française has facilitated many activities including scholarship opportunities.

Student exchanges, both to and from Sarasota, have taken place in 1996-1997, followed closely by additional exchanges in 1998 and another set of exchanges in 2009-2010 between Pablo Picasso Lycee and Riverview High School students. The last trip had a Solar Energy theme and SCAS received a $1,000 Sustainable Development Award for the program from the Department of Energy and an Innovation Award in Sustainability from Sister Cities International.

Students from Perpignan Pablo Picasso Lycee with Perpignan teacher Hadda LaMotte posing with Riverview High School students

In 2008, an invitation was extended from our Perpignan Sister City to send a delegation of eight Sarasota High School students to Perpignan to participate in their famous Catalan Festival. The students were charged with creating their own performance in competition with students from the other six Perpignan sister cities of Leida, Spain; Maalot-Tarshiha, Israel; Tavira, Portugal; Hanover, Germany; Lancaster, England and Tyre, Lebanon.

Students from all the Sarasota area high schools were invited to apply for the competition and Perpignan City Director Harry Dunn, Asst. Director Eva Frank and VP-Education Ray Young interviewed all the applicants. Selection was based on their involvement in performing and fine arts, maturity, poise, ability to speak diplomatically and how they expressed their views of their own culture.

The students selected to represent SCAS at the festival are shown in the picture below and were from Pineview HS, Cardinal Mooney, the Out-of-Door Academy and Riverview HS. Jim Shirley the Director of Development for PAL Sailor Circus (at the time) and his wife Barbara volunteered to serve as chaperones for the team of students. On their own, the students composed the performance on site and won the competition!

Sarasota High School Students (l to r) Christian Keller, Christy Skarulis, Calliope Desenberg, Shanley Caswell, Nina Danese, Amber Sulesky, Mary Kelly,
Alex Shames is identified in the photo below

Students having lunch in Perpignan, Alex Shames is third from left and Chaperone Jim Shirley is at the end of the table.
Shanley Caswell in top photo is now a noted Hollywood actress best known for her starring role in the movie "Detention" in 2011.

Catalan Festival Performances

In 2011, Perpignan invited a SCAS delegation to meet with the mayor and other city officials and spend a week learning about Perpignan. The delegation was given front row seats to the inauguration of the new National Theatre Archipelago that had just been completed in Perpignan as shown below.

National Theatre Archipelago

Several art exchanges have occurred with Perpignan. An early one was a digital art exchange between the Ecole Supérieure D'Art De Perpignan and the Manatee Community College (now State College of Florida). It was designated as a "Blue Exchange" with all the art in blue tones.

Young women with Blue Hair

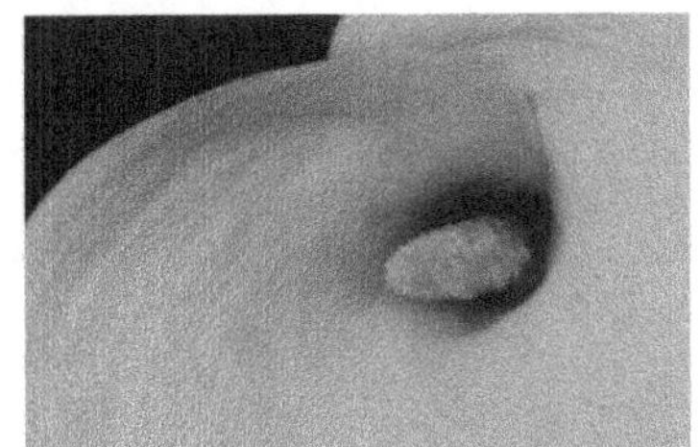

Intense Blue Flower

In 2015, the Art Center of Sarasota featured twenty emerging artists from the Perpignan area in a month-long exhibit entitled "Confluence-France." A VIP reception was held for SCAS and Alliance Francaise members on opening night, followed by the general public.

SCAS VP Gloria Grenier, President Beth Ruyle and the Sarasota Art Center
Director at opening of "Confluence-France" Art show

Early in the development of the sister city relationship with Perpignan, a film exchange was negotiated whereby French films were sent for audience viewing in Sarasota. This became the precursor of the now annual Sarasota Film Festival with showing of significant Hollywood and international films, gatherings and visitations by noted actors and actresses.

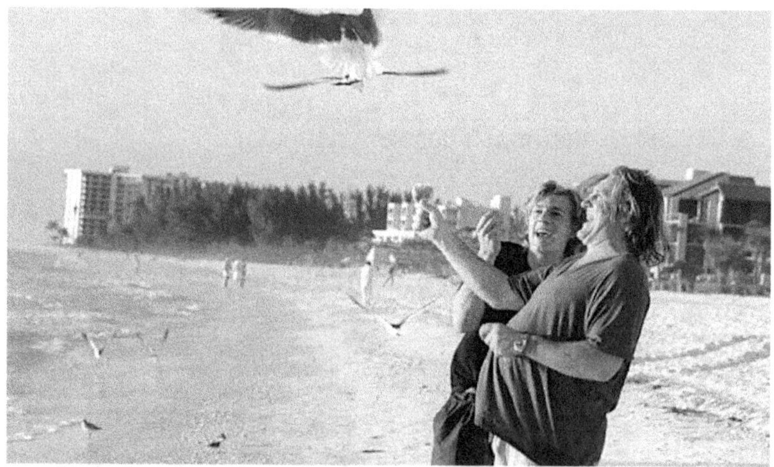

French actor Gerard and Guillaume Depardieu
frolicking on Siesta Beach during Sarasota Film Festival

Vladimir, Russia (1994)

The twinning with Vladimir was promoted by members of the Sarasota Rotary Club. Vladimir wanted to establish a Rotary Club and needed a sponsor. The Sarasota Rotary Club volunteered, establishing the connection. A delegation traveled to Vladimir after the official signing and helped establish the club in Vladimir.

SCAS delegation visit to Vladimir shows (l to r) Mayor Richard Martin, the Docent to Suzdal Historical Village and Commissioner Lou Ann Palmer.

After meeting Yelena Bychkovskikh, a Vladimir city employee involved in international relations, Mayor Lou Ann Palmer invited her to Sarasota and became a mentor for the young woman who enrolled as an advanced degree student at the University of Florida.

Sarasota Mayor Richard Martin presenting keys to city to Vladimir student Yelena Bychkovskikh accompanied by mentor and former mayor Lou Ann Palmer at Sister City luncheon in Sarasota.

Vladimir students have frequently been chosen as winners in the Florida Studio Theatre's annual Young Playwrights competition. They have visited Sarasota to be honored and see their plays presented by professional actors as further described in the Joint Programs section.

An early digital art exchange was arranged between the Vladimir Pedagogical University in Vladimir and the Manatee Community College (now State College of Florida). Some of the artwork displayed at the colleges is shown below.

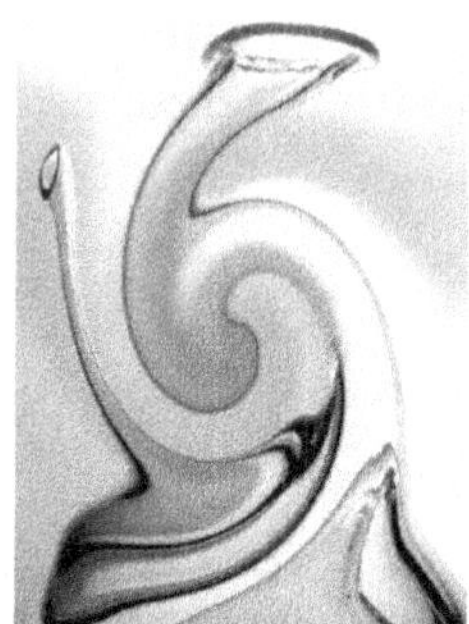

In 2012, a delegation led by Vladimir Police Chief, Alexander Rasov, visited Sarasota to meet with local law enforcement and discuss and compare approaches to security and methods of implementation.

Mayor Susan Atwell exchanging gifts with
Vladimir Police Chief, Alexander Rasov

City Director Yulia Glaukman and her husband Alex lead an exchange to Vladimir in 2013, with trips to Moscow, St Petersburg and Suzdal. The SCAS group was graciously hosted by Russian families in their homes.

SCAS Delegation in Vladimir with Vladimir Mayor (4th from right) and Chief of Police (2nd from right)

SCAS Delegation with Vladimir Theater Performers

In the fall of 2019, City Director Miriam Kramer traveled with a Sister Cities International (SCI) delegation to Moscow for the Fifth Municipal Conference. She then visited our Sister City of Vladimir, and the neighboring city of Suzdal to establish ties with our counterparts there. Her counterparts, the teachers and tour guides Tatiana and Marina Semenova of Vladimir, were tremendously cooperative and supportive of our projects and exchanges.

A performance by local Russians with one performer shown at left at an SCAS luncheon, (l to r) Russian dancer, long-time supporters of SCAS Richard Mantyla and Vicky Swenson and Vladimir City Director Yulia Glaukman

With Vladimir City Representative Roman Aleksandrov, Vladimir City Director Miriam Kramer organized the inaugural online chess tournament between our Sarasota Chess Club and the Chess Club Vladimir. The tournament was very well received and plans are in the works to hold another chess tournament soon.

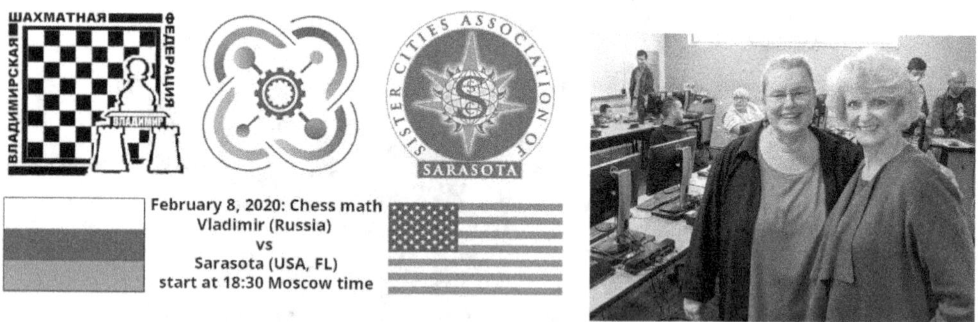

Former Presidents Miriam Kramer and Beth-Ruyle Hullinger
at Chess Match library site in Sarasota

Tel Mond, Israel (1999)

The 10th anniversary ceremony was conducted in Tel Mond by a delegation led by Mayor Lou Ann Palmer and Commissioner Ken Shelin. Sarasota has had a long history of intense interaction with Tel Mond through many prominent Sarasota citizens as well as the Sarasota-Manatee Jewish Federation that helped in the development of this vibrant city. Tel Mond's impressive arts and education program is evidenced in the submissions to elementary school art projects that involved all of Sarasota sister cities. In 1997, four Sarasota high school students, including one from the Sarasota Sailor Circus traveled to Tel Mond for a youth exchange.

Noted Sarasota Philanthropist Betty Schoenbaum also donated a library to Tel Mond that furthered our strong ties to the city.

Sarasota Mayor Willie Shaw with Philanthropist Betty Schoenbaum

The Tel Mond Regional Library donated by Betty and Alex Schoenbaum
Shown (l to r) Susan Rosin, Linda Rosenbluth, Esther Razabi and Lou Ann Palmer

Tel Mond has participated in many cross cultural visits over the years, including Boy Scouts, the award-winning Video Boot Camp, the Sister City International Art Show and the International Photography competition. Youngsters from Tel Mond have won Florida Studio Theater's Young Playwrights competition multiple times.

High School dancers and singers from Tel Mond have visited and performed in Sarasota in 2005, 2012 and 2015. Venues have included the Riverview HS auditorium, the Sarasota Military Academy and the Jewish Federation.

Young women dancers from Tel Mond performing in Sarasota.

Tel Mond Singers performing in Sarasota

A delegation from SCAS toured Israel and visited with the mayor of Tel Mond and made several school visits in April, 2014. Recognition was given to the many students from Tel Mond who had been winners in the Sarasota Young Playwright Competition further described below in the section on Joint Sister Cities Programs.

Presentation of certificates by SCAS delegation to students in Tel Mond in 2014 (l to r), SCAS VP-Education Ray Young, Tel Mond Major Ronnie Golan, SCAS President Beth Ruyle-Hullinger and Tel Mond City Director Linda Rosenbluth

Tel Mond was the first Sarasota Sister City to have a song written about the relationship between the two cities. Sid Krupkin, a SCAS member, and Elie Matstree of Tel Mond combined to compose "Sarasota and Tel Mond" which features their musical talents combined with singing by school children from both cities.

Asst City Director Alice Cotman with Sidney Krupkin who composed a song about the sister city with Elie Matstree. Listen to the song at: sistercitysongs.blogspot.com

SCAS Delegation visit to Tel Mond in April, 2014
led by Linda Rosenbluth (5th from right)
Also in the group are Fred Bloom, Sue Rosin, Craig Hullinger, Ray Young, Beth Ruyle,
Leone Levy, Vickie Swenson and Richard Mantyla

Dunfermline, Scotland (2002)

SCAS linked several Sarasota institutions together with Dunfermline programs since the official signing at the Van Wezel Performing Arts Center. Links were established between Lauder College of Dunfermline and Manatee Community College (MCC) (now State College of Florida) and between St Leonards School, Dunfermline and Pineview HS. A Lauder College Digital Art Exhibit was created for the opening of the Center for Innovation Technology at MCC and photographs by David Ewles of Dunfermline were also displayed at the Selby Library in Sarasota.

An exchange of Boy Scouts and Girl Scouts between the sister cities was instituted in 2008. Large delegations of Sarasota Girl Scouts went to Dunfermline and Dunfermline Boy Scouts to Sarasota. It was a very exciting for the young people to experience the new different cultures of the sister cities.

Sarasota Girl Scouts in Dunfermline in 2008

The 10th Anniversary of this twinning was held at the Silver Thistle Ball at the Bird Bay Yacht Club in Sarasota in 2012, jointly sponsored by the Caledonian Club of West Florida and the Sister Cities Association of Sarasota. The event featured the Riverview High School 'Kiltie Band" and, of course, toasts of native scotch libation. Also in 2012 the Key Chorale of Sarasota gave a performance in Carnegie Hall in Dunfermline.

Dunfermline Boy Scouts in Sarasota
hosted by City Director Bill Wallace (left front)

Members of SCAS were thrilled to know that their very own tartan honoring ties
with Dunfermline had been designed and produced for use as kilts, scarfs, etc.
Shown below are former City Director Bill Wallace and Don Osborne displaying
the special tartan. The carefully chosen colors of the plaid are gold for the sun and
teal for our coastal waters; blue designates the color heralded by Dunfermline and
white for all of our sister cities.

Bill Wallace and Don Osborne with SCAS Tartan

An SCAS delegation visit to Dunfermline and other areas of Scotland took place in
2016. During the visit the delegation was met by the Deputy Provost Kay Morrison
for a civic reception at the city Chamber of Commerce. At the reception a film
about the move of the old Dunfermline Opera House to Sarasota for reconstruction
as the Merck Theater was shown to the SCAS delegation and the producers were

introduced to our members. During the visit the SCAS delegation was given a tour of the new modern library in the city and the Carnegie home and library.

SCAS Delegation visit to Dunfermline in 2016, front row (l to r)
SCAS President Beth Ruyle-Hullinger, Dunfermline Deputy Provost Kay Morrison
and Dunfermline City Director Pauline Mitchell

Sarasota Key Chorale performing in Dunfermline Carnegie Hall.

After a performance by a Scottish high school band during the SCAS visit to Dunfermline, SCAS member Fred Bloom invited one of the young bagpipers to Sarasota to perform with the Riverview High School 'Kiltie Band." The performance was held in the Riverview auditorium to an appreciative audience of 100 people.

Young Scottish bagpiper who performed in Sarasota flanked by all the previous winners from Dunfermline of the Sarasota Young Playwright Competition over many years. The sponsoring Dunfermline teachers are also shown in the photo.

The famous Scottish metal sculptor, Malcolm Robertson, makes his winter home in Sarasota and his sculptures can be seen in both Scotland and in Sarasota at the Fruitville Library and the traffic circle on south Manasota Key.

Each year Sarasota Sister Cities supports the **Sarasota Highland Games** in honor of our Scottish Sister City, Dunfermline. Each Clan as well as Sarasota Sister Cities maintain a booth to inform people about our organization. The games include all kinds of traditional Scottish feats of strength. Pauline Mitchell has led our efforts for 19 years, and the event is fun and worthwhile.

SCAS Board members march proudly in parade at the Highlands Games in Sarasota

Treviso, Italy (2007) (emeritus)

The twinning resulted in a rich, active exchange program aided by interest of alliance organizations such as the Ausonia Society and Sarasota Italian Cultural Events.

The official signing delegation from Treviso included the major, city officials and a master chef who had shipped in all the food from Italy for the signing celebration in Sarasota. The lavish dinner was prepared by the Treviso chef to the delight of all in attendance.

A digital art exchange took place between fine art students in Treviso and Sarasota in 2008. Digital art was transferred between students from the Liceo Artistico Statale di Treviso and Manatee Community College (Now State College of Florida) and displayed at the respective institutions.

The Director of the Ringling Museum of Art, John Wetenhall, traveled to Treviso to meet with museum directors to establish future exchanges. This was followed by the Sarasota Key Chorale giving a performance in Treviso in 2009.

Sarasota Key Chorale performance in Treviso in 2009

The winner of our 2009 People and Places Photography Contest involving all our Sister Cities was Treviso artist Cristina Madeyski with her "Magic Reflections - Treviso on the Sile River" entry. The winning photograph is shown in the section below on joint sister city programs. This led to a subsequent showing of her work at the Selby Auditorium on the University of South Florida Sarasota-Manatee campus in February 2012.

Art show of work by Treviso artist Cristina Madeyski at USF-Sarasota/Manatee. On left is Treviso City Director Alexandra DeStefanis, 3rd from left is Cristina Madeyski, 4th is former CD-Treviso Susanna Wriston and 2nd from right is Gayle Maxey.

Sarasota Sister City Delegation on steps of Collato Castle in the Alpine foothills of Sister City Treviso Province in 2010

Siming District, Xiamen, China (2007)

A ten person delegation traveled to Xiamen for the official signing ceremony. This included Mayor Lou Ann Palmer and sister city representatives Linda Rosenbluth, Hope Byrnes and Raymond Young. The reception by the Chinese hosts was exquisite and gracious.

Former VP-Education Ray Young being greeted with welcoming hand-shake on arrival in Xiamen, China; along with former SCAS Presidents Hope Burns (l) and Linda Rosenbluth (r). Xiamen representatives subsequently visited Sarasota.

Informal gathering of SCAS delegation to China
(l to r) Former SCAS President Hope Burns, Siming (Xiamen) Official, Sarasota
Mayor Lou Ann Palmer, Xiamen City Director Carolyn Bloomer,
Former SCAS President Linda Rosenbluth, SCAS VP-Education Raymond Young

The art work of a fourth grade student from Xiamen, Luo Sihang (below), was selected for the grand prize of $1,000 in the Embracing our Differences exhibit in Bayfront Park in Sarasota in 2008. She received high praise and coverage for her achievement in the Chinese press.

At the same time in 2008 that Lou Sihang's art was on display in Sarasota, eleven high-level officials from Xiamen visited Sarasota. The delegation included Mayor Pan Shijian and the Directors of Municipal Bureaus of Urban Planning, Civil Administration, Sports, Ocean & Fisheries, Foreign Affairs, Transportation and Tourism. Mayor Shijian had a special interest in public art, especially sculpture. Members of the Gulf Coast Chinese American Association and the Sarasota chapter of the U.S. China People's Friendship Association also greeted the Xiamen delegation.

An "Exchange of Artists" program was begun in 2009 when Sarasota hosted two artists from China for two weeks. In May, 2011, two local artists, Robert Farber and Julio Rodriguez, were chosen by a panel of local jurors to travel to Xiamen for two weeks where they, too, were hosted by local families and experienced the Chinese art community.

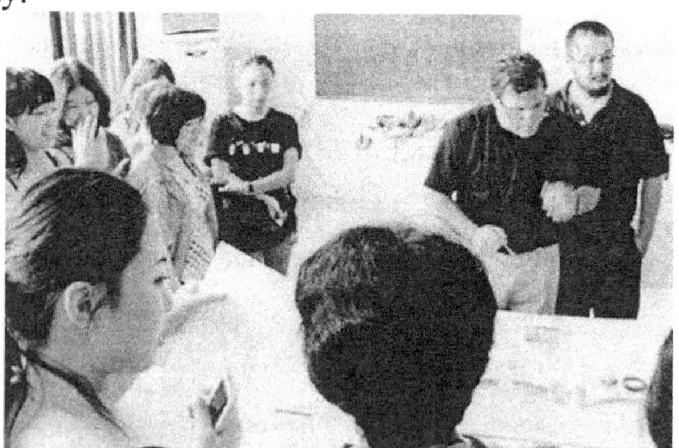

SCAS sponsored visiting artist Robert Farber demonstrating work for students in Xiamen, China as part of artist exchange program.

Exchange of exhibitions of art and photography have also been held between the Fujian Arts & Craft College and Xiamen University and the Ringling College of Art & Design and the Manatee Community College (now State College of Florida).

Merida, Mexico (2010)

Several SCAS delegations have visited Merida on several occasions. The Latino Excellence of Sarasota, an alliance member of SCAS, conducted a custom exchange tour in July 2012. It provided a unique opportunity to experience Mayan life and ancient cities in the region of Merida. The guided tour featured intimate experiences including participation in sacred Maya ceremonies with Mayan priests and healers.

A five member delegation of four Businessmen and the Chief of Police of Merida visited Sarasota and were greeted by Mayor Willie Shaw in City Hall. The group explored opportunities for joint business ventures particularly related to Marine Enterprises.

Merida delegate of business men exchange gifts with Mayor Willie Shaw (center) hosted by City Director Mike Fehily (2nd from left)

An Economic Development Meeting between representatives of Sarasota and Merida was held in Sarasota in December, 2019. SCAS was represented by Mike Fehily, Grisell Aleman, Craig Hullinger, Philip Gordon and Toni Duval, the City of Sarasota by Steve Stancil of the Sarasota Economic Development Program and for Merida was Julio Sauma Castillo, Secretary of the Department of Community

Outreach. The discussion ranged from economic development incentives, trade and investment between the two cities, grant programs, improved tourism, redevelopment agencies, and better transportation between the two cities.

Economic Development Meeting between representatives of Sarasota and Merida. (l to r) Steve Stancil, Julio Sauma Castillo, Grisell Aleman, Mike Fehily, and Philip Gordon

Merida Secretary of the Department of Community Outreach Julio Sauma Castillo Meets with Mayor Jen Ahearn-Koch at City Hall

Mayor Willie Shaw, City Director Mike Fehily, and President Beth Ruyle held a confirmation signing of the Sister City relationship with Merida in 2019 and a virtual revalidation was held in 2020 between Merida Mayor Renan Berra Concha, Sarasota Mayor Hagen Brody and SCAS President Toni Duval.

In August, 2023 City Director Grisell Aleman traveled to Merida to discuss future plans, specifically initiatives for university student exchanges between Merida and Sarasota. The mayor of Merida is very keen on pursuing this plan. Shown below is Grisell meeting and exchanging gifts in Merida.

Mariana Valle, Director of Special Projects for Merida (l to r), Jose Luis Marinez Semerena, Director of Economic Development and Tourism of Merida County and Grisell Aleman, City Director for Merida.

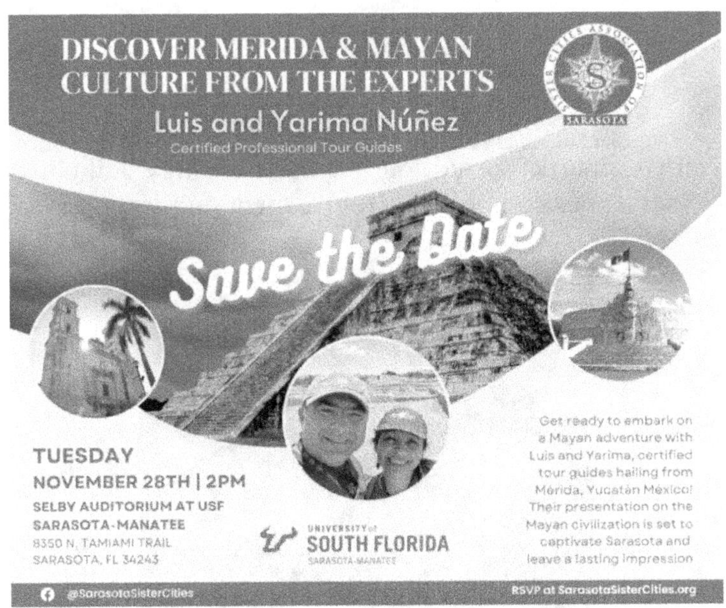

An SCAS sponsored event about Mayan culture at the University of South Florida in Sarasota

Rapperswil-Jona, Switzerland
Friendship City (2014) (emeritus)

Exchanges with Rapperswil-Jona (R-J) began not long after the signing ceremony. A group of four young volleyball players arrived in Sarasota to compete in a volleyball tournament on Siesta Key. They were hosted by City Director Nelly Camardo who toured them through Sarasota. This was followed by a visit of the Dean of University of Applied Science (HSR Technical College) in R-J to Sarasota. Nelly Camardo and Raymond Young escorted Dean Alex Simeon to Ringling College and University of South Florida-Sarasota/Manatee where he explored possible exchanges of faculty and students.

City Director Nelly Camardo hosted four handsome volley ball players who visited Sarasota to compete in a tournament on Siesta Key.

University of Applied Science in foreground and town of R-J in background

Busseto, Italy Friendship City (2019)

Busseto is the historic home of the great Maestro Giuseppe Verdi. Sarasota Maestero Victor DeRenzi was very keen on establishing Busetto as a sister city. In 1989 Maestro DeRenzi began The Verdi Cycle—a unique undertaking to perform the complete works of Giuseppe Verdi. The 2016 Winter Opera Festival marked the grand finale of this extraordinary journey with productions of Aida and The Battle of Legnano. The final week was devoted exclusively to the Italian master, that included concerts of his music, talks, panel discussions, and other special events. The completion of the Cycle has made Sarasota Opera the only company in the world to have performed all of Verdi's music!

City Director Phillip Gordon made frequent contacts with the Mayor of Busseto and learned that the historic home of Giuseppe Verdi had fallen into disrepair. In 2021, the SCAS Board of Director voted to make a $5,000 contribution to the funding to restore Verdi's historic home.

In 2022 Assistant City Director Dennis Ciborowski visited Busetto to present a gift of a letter from Sarasota Mayor Erik Arroyo and a commemorative plaque from SCAS and the city of Sarasota to the Mayor of Busseto, Sindaco Stefano Nevicati, at the Villa Verdi in Busseto. Later in 2022, City Director Jeanne Murphy also visited Busseto to develop future plans with the city officials.

Historic Villa Verdi built in 1848 in Hamlet of Sant'Agata di Vilanova

ACD Dennis Ciborowski presenting gifts to Busseto Mayor Nevicati

Joint Sister City Projects and Exchanges

Joint Sister City activities are those held in Sarasota that involve more than one sister city. The joint projects and exchanges are more festive and interactive since more people are involved from a variety of cultures. We have had a number of these projects with as many as six of our sister cities representatives at one time in Sarasota.

Multicultural Sister City gathering in Sarasota
for the 100th Anniversary of the Founding of Sarasota
Standing (l to r) - Perpignan Delegate Dominique Villain, Perpignan Deputy Mayor Maurice Halimi, SCAS VP-Economic Development John Brown, Treviso CD Susanna Wriston, Dunfermline Delegate Grant Ward, Tel Mond Delegate Moshe Babel-Pour, Treviso Delegate S. Leonardo Muraro;
Seated – Perpignan Delegate Mme. Halimi and Tel Mond CD Alice Cotman, 2002

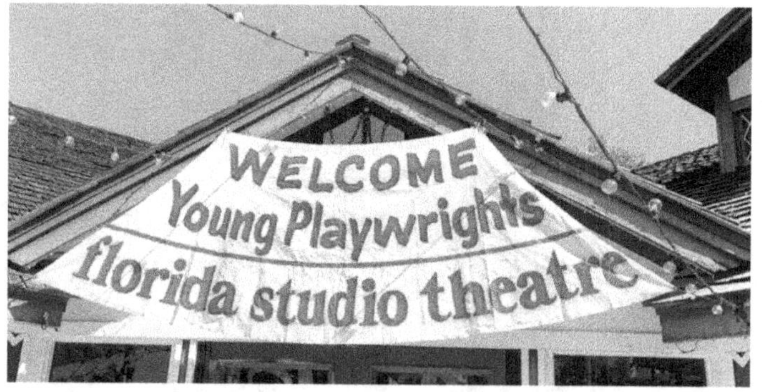

Write a Play Competition and Young Playwrights Festival

One of the significant joint projects is the "Write a Play Competition and Young Playwrights Festival" offered jointly with the Florida Studio Theatre. Entries of short plays composed by young playwrights are received in two categories, elementary and high school level students. The plays are evaluated by a panel of judges composed of members of FSU and SCAS and the winning playwrights from our sister cities are invited to Sarasota to watch their plays performed by professional actors on stage during the Young Playwrights Festival. SCAS hosts the students for about a week further exposing them to other cultural and educational amenities in Sarasota.

The students engage in local activities, sightseeing and meeting government officials. The FST Young Playwrights Program has been led by Linda Rosenbluth, Gloria Grenier and Sue Gordon. There have been over 40 winners of the competition since 2004 from our sister cities of Dunfermline, Tel Mond, Vladimir and Xiamen.

Young Playwright recipients from Dunfermline and Tel Mond

Young Playwrights receiving awards
from Mayor Susan Atwell in City Hall

Professional FST Actors

In 2016 teachers from three of our sister cities were invited to Sarasota for a special training session on playwriting. The training was conducted by Adam Ratner and Caroline Kaiser at the Florida Studio Theater to further promote the Young Playwrights Competition for our sister cities.

Sister Cities teachers receiving citations from Sarasota Mayor Liz Alpert at City Hall (l to r). Hadda LaMotte from Perpignan, Idit Levy from Tel Mond, Mayor Alpert, SCAS President Marianna Janz-Wecke and Elisa Carollo from Teviso Italy.

Tri-City Baseball Tournament

A joint program was initiated very early in the history of SCAS, not long after the formation of the organization. The "Tri-City Baseball Tournament" was held in 1964 and included competition between the Sarasota American Legion baseball team, a Hamilton High School baseball team and a team from Santo Domingo. The teams competed at the professional league Ed Smith Baseball Stadium in Sarasota.

Sarasota Sister Cities Video Boot Camp

The Video Boot Camp joint project was held in 1998. The program involved twenty students from Santo Domingo, Hamilton, Perpignan, Vladimir, Tel Mond and Sarasota. The project was a hands-on introduction to video production and broadcast journalism. The event was organized by Linda Rosenbluth of SCAS and Dan Kennedy of Sarasota High School.

Students from Santo Domingo, Hamilton, Perpignan, Vladimir, Tel Mond and Sarasota with Sarasota HS Principal Dan Kennedy at Video Boot Camp.

Hands of Heritage Fest

A Heritage Fest was held in 2003 at the Sarasota Robarts Arena. Booths were set up to display characteristic materials and art from each our sister cities.

Director of Events Gayle Maxey, President Linda Rosenbluth, member Morton Stich and Barbara Hamilton discuss some of the student artwork on display at the Hands of Heritage Festival at Robarts Arena

Some of the art submitted by young students from Perpignan, Tel Mond and Vladimir are shown below:

Perpignan

Tel Mond

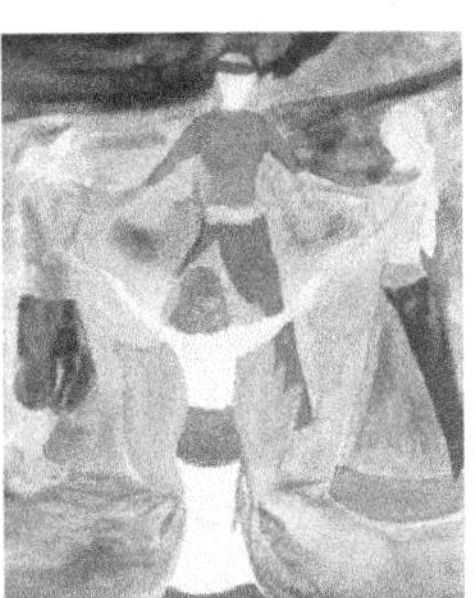

Vladimir

International Photo Contest Exhibition of People & Places

An "International Photo Contest and Exhibition of People and Places" was sponsored by SCAS in 2009. Digital images from all of our sister cities at the time were submitted for the contest. A total of sixty photos from Dunfermline, Hamilton, Vladimir, Xiamen, Treviso and Perpignan were selected and mounted, framed and displayed at the Ringling College of Art and Design, Manatee Community College, University of South Florida-Sarasota/Manatee, City Hall and Sarasota Libraries.

The photos were a powerful statement of the goals and objectives of SCAS to develop respect, understanding and cooperation through citizen diplomacy. The exhibit was organized and executed by Kim Sheintal and Greg Carlson.

Photo Contest winner was "Magic Reflections-Treviso on the Sile River" by Treviso artist Cristina Madeyski

International Sustainability Conference

A joint project that involved six of sister cities in Sarasota was the "Sustainability Through Renewable Energy & Aquaculture Conference" held on the campus of the University of South Florida-Sarasota/Manatee in 2013. The conference was attended by 300 people from SCAS, college and high school students, university faculty and many members from the community.

University of South Florida-Sarasota/Manatee

There were 25 presenters representing six of our sister cities, ten different university and college programs in Florida, two national organizations, one international institution and several private renewable energy companies. A special poster session was held at the venue where students from four Sarasota high schools displayed their projects. The conference brochure is shown in the subsequent section containing SCAS brochures.

Student Sustainability Posters presented at the SCAS International Sustainability\
Conference at USF-Sarasota/Manatee

The six sister cities speakers at the Sustainability Conference and their presentation topics are given below. The conference was organized by VP-Education, Raymond Young, supported by a committee of Harry Dunn, Gloria Grenier, Dave Harralson, John Buecheler, USF Dean Jane Rose and other representatives of USF.

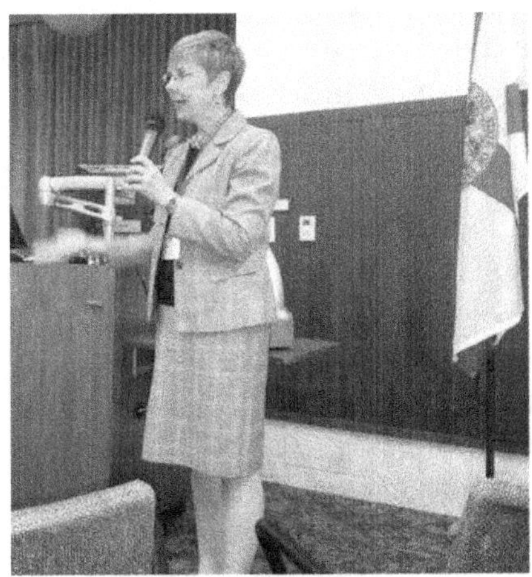

USF Dean Jane Rose provided the opening remarks for the SCAS International Conference on Sustainability Through Renewable Energy & Aquaculture

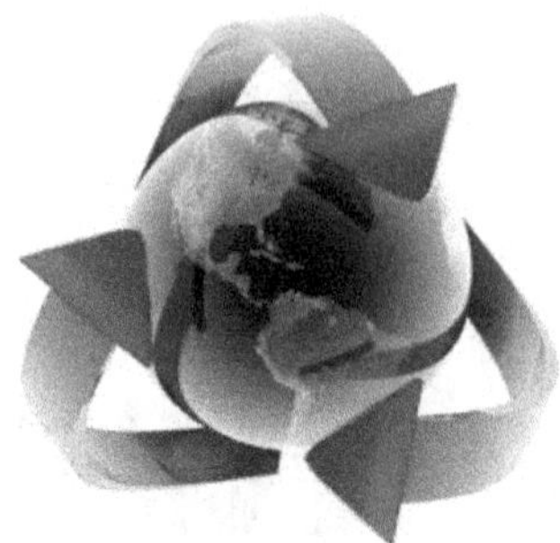

Sarasota Sister City International Presentations at
Conference on Sustainability Through Renewable Energy & Aquaculture

<u>Sustainability</u>
    Programs for Sustainable Buildings in Treviso Province, Italy
        Antonio Zonta
        Treviso Province Administration
        Treviso, Italy
    Improving the Quality of Desalinated Seawater
        Professor Ori Lahav
        Technion, Israel Institute of Technology
        Tel Mond/Haifa, Israel
<u>Renewable Energy Alternatives</u>
    Solar Energy Storage
        Professor Xavier Py
        University of Perpignan
        Perpignan, France
    Facing the Energy Skills Challenge
        Professor Sandy Murray
        Carnegie College & Whitlock Energy Collaboration Center
        Dunfermline, Scotland
<u>Sustainability of Ocean Resources</u>
    The Yucatan Fishery Resources: Trends & Perspectives to Sustainability
        Professor Carlos Gonzalez-Salas & Professor Humberto Cervera
        Autonomous University of the Yucatan
        Merida, Mexico
    Characteristics & Development Trends of China's Fisheries & Aquaculture
        Dr. Qian Ma
        Yellow Sea Fisheries Research Institute
        Qingdao/Xiamen, China

Additional information about the Sustainability Conference available at:
https://sustainablesarasota.blogspot.com

Another unique type project involving all of our sister cities was organized by Miriam Kramer who had ties with the Barnes & Nobles Book Store in Sarasota. The event was the **"Sarasota Sister Cities Book Fair."** The goal was to both raise community awareness of SCAS and raise additional funds for SCAS at the bookstore event. Books representing each of our sister cities were sold at the Book Fair with a portion of the proceeds for SCAS. The books are worth listing below for future reference.

Vladimir Russia
"A Gentleman in Moscow" by Amor Towles
"Red Fortunes" by Hugh Fraser
"A Bend in the Stars" by Rachel Barenbaum

Tel Mond, Israel
"Star-up Nation: The Story of Israel's Economic Miracle"
    by Dan Senor & Saul Singer
"Israel from Above" by Hanit Armonn & Itamar Grinberg
"Promised Land: A Novel of Israel" by Martin Fletcher

Merida, Mexico
"The Jungle of the Stone" by William Carlsen
"Yucatan by David Sterling (Ultimate book on Mayan and Yucatan recipes but an
    also an excellent history of Merida and all of the Yucatan), multiple awards

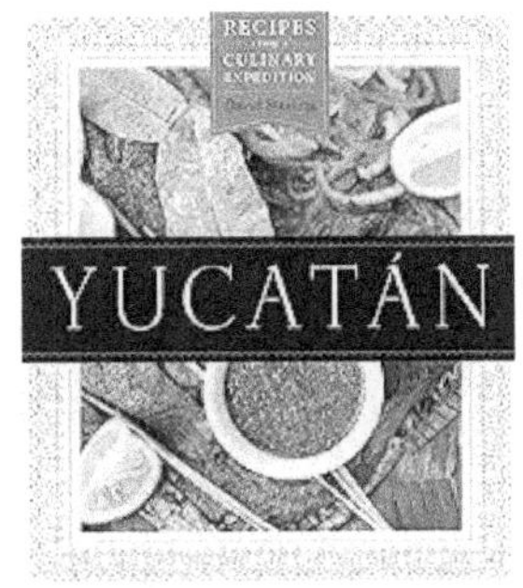

Busseto, Italy
"Life of Verdi" by John Rosselli
"The Man Verdi" by Frank Walker
"Verdi: A Biography" by Mary Jane Phillips-Matz
"Amarcord: Marcella Remembers" by Marcella Hazan
"The Faithful: A Novel Based on the Life of Giuseppe Verdi" by Collin Mitchell

Dunfermline, Scotland
"Carnegie's Maid" by Marie Benedict
"The Outlander Series" by Diana Gabaldon
"Knots & Crosses" by Ian Rankin
"The Lady of the Lake" by Sir Walter Scott

Xiamen, China
"China" by Patricia Buckley Ebrey
"An Illustrated History of Modern China" by Jeffrey N. Wasserstrom
"China in the 21st Century: What Everyone Needs to Know"
    by J. Wasserstrom & M. Cunningham
"China's New Red Guards" by Jude D. Blanchette

Perpignan
"Languedoc Roussillon Tarn Gorges: Travel Guide" Michelin Green Guides
"The Cathars" by Malcolm Barber
"Fauves and Fauvism" by Jean Leymarie

Community Events and Activities

Sarasota Sister Cities conducts a wide range of community activities. The following highlights our Luncheons, Speakers Bureau, One World Awards, Annual Gala, Embracing Our Differences, Festival-4-Life, Trolley Tours, Promotional Events and Meet & Greets.

Luncheons

Monthly luncheons have been a major feature for SCAS for many years. The luncheons feature a prominent speaker on topics relevant both to our local community and the international scene. Frequently a Sister City Director will provide a description and update of events, exchanges and trips to their sister city. Presidents and leaders of significant community organizations are also often invited speakers to the luncheons. In recent years the luncheons have been held at the Bird Key Yacht Club in Sarasota.

SCAS President Toni Duval introducing Maestro Victor DeRenzi for luncheon presentation at the Bird Key Yacht Club.

<u>A few examples of community related luncheon presentations:</u>
Future of New College of Florida
       Dr. Patricia Okker, President, New College of Florida
Circus Arts Conservatory - Sailor Circus
       Jennifer Mitchell, VP/COO
Embracing our Differences Program
       Sarah Wertheimer, Executive Director
Friendship Center Programs - People Helping People
       Robert Rogers, Director of Community Outreach
Perspectives on Marie Selby Botanical Gardens
       Jennifer Rominiecki, President & CEO

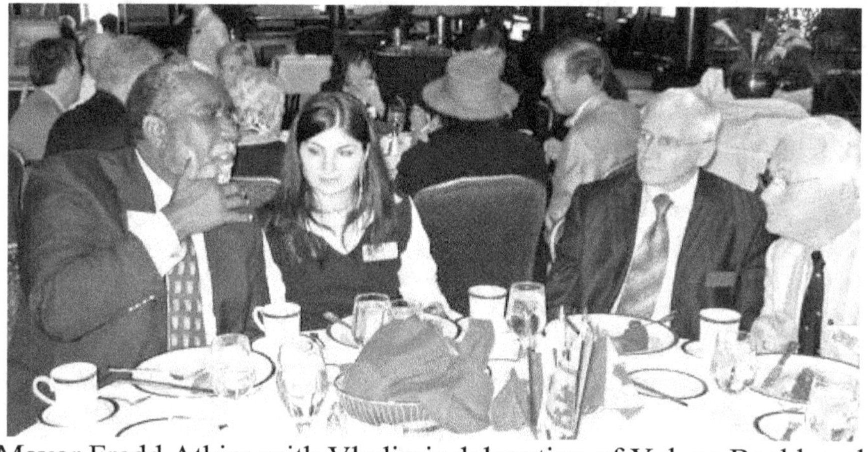Mary Jean Eisenhower granddaughter of President Dwight D. Eisenhower, founder of the people to people program, provided a presentation at the SCAS luncheon in 2003.

Former Mayor Fredd Atkins with Vladimir delegation of Yelena Bychkovskikh and Mayor Alexander Rybakov at 2007 luncheon honoring the Russian mayor.

Ringling Museum Director Steven High taking questions from audience after
presentation on future programs at the museum
with SCAS President Miriam Kramer.

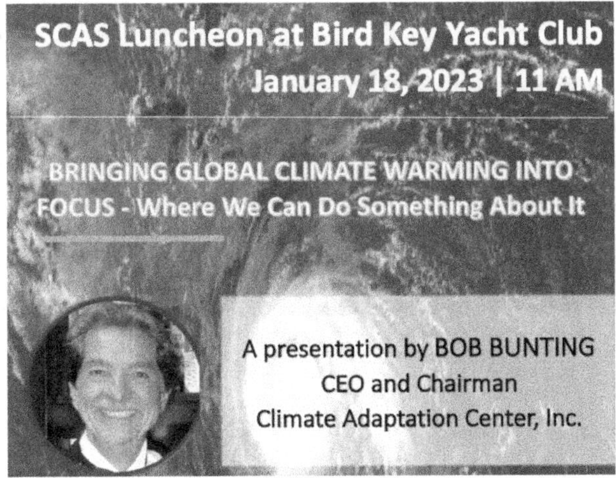

SCAS Luncheon "Honoring the Mayors of Sarasota"

Building Bridges of Peace and Understanding

Sister Cities Association of Sarasota Mayoral Luncheon
March 20, 2019
Bird Key Yacht Club

Excerpt from the Sarasota Herald-Tribune, May, 2019

"The luncheon menu, a tribute to each of the Sister Cities, inspired table conversation and storytelling about the importance of citizen-to-citizen diplomacy and exchanges between Sarasota and its nine Sister Cities. The program was hosted by SCAS VP Communications Toni Duval and VP Education Dr. Raymond Young, who shared the "Sarasota Sister Cities Story" in pictures highlighting the mayors' involvement with Sister City "twining" and other exchanges. Sister Cities organizations nationwide create city-to-city programs which establish linkages and foster friendships among citizens around the world. SCAS coordinates arts, economic, sports and other people-to-people exchanges with its Sister Cities."

Official "Honoring Our Mayors" Luncheon Attendees (l to r)
Mayor Elmer Birkel, Pres. Hope Byrnes, Pres. Carla Rayman, Mayor Shellie Freedland Eddie, Mayor Liz Alpert, Mayor Mollie Cardamone, Mayor Rita Roehr, Pres. Tom Halbert, Major Richard Clapp, Mayor Fredd Atkins

SCAS Luncheon "Honoring the Past Presidents of SCAS"

A special luncheon was held in 2017 to honor the former presidents of SCAS. All the former presidents still available in Sarasota were invited to the presentation and included Wells Purmort, Hope Burns, Linda Rosenbluth, Bill Wallace, Carla Rayman, Tom Halbert, Beth Ruyle-Hullinger. VP Raymond Young highlighted the contributions of each of the presidents during their term in office in a powerpoint presentation. Embossed plaques were then awarded to each former president. All of the former SCAS presidents are listed in an above section and a short biographical sketch for recent presidents is included in the Biographies section of book.

SCAS Presidents at tribute luncheon (l to r), Bill Wallace, Tom Halbert, Linda Rosenbluth, Hope Byrnes, Beth Ruyle, Wells Purmort and Carla Rayman.

Plaques awarded to each of our SCAS Presidents at the luncheon

Below are Presidents that have served after the luncheon honoring the past presidents of SCAS.

Marianna Janz-Wecke

Toni Duval

Miriam Kramer

Diana Friedman

Sarasota Sister Cities Speakers Bureau

The SCAS Speakers Bureau was originally conceived and organized by VP-Communications Craig Hullinger and VP-Education Ray Young with the idea of featuring a wide range of community and sister city presentations. The monthly presentations have now been offered for over ten years first at the auditorium in the Herald-Tribune Bldg on Main St. and later at the Gelbart Auditorium at the Sarasota Selby Library where they continue today. The excellent presentations have provided a great forum for provoking questions and lively conservation. Each presentation is followed by a "Happy Hour, Meet & Greet" gathering at a local restaurant for continued discussion by members of the audience. It has been a very successful and entertaining program.

<u>Example of some previous presentations in the Speakers Bureau Program</u>
International Travel & Culture
France: A Tale of Two Cities: Paris and Perpignan
    Emile Langlois, Barbara Frey & Gloria Grenier
Firth of Forth in Fife - Scotland and Dunfermline
    Pauline Mitchell
China Behind the Travel Posters
    Carolyn Bloomer Ph.D.
Polynesian Cultures of the South Pacific
    Raymond Young, Ph.D.
Perspectives on Treviso and Italy
    Susanna Wriston
Global Body Language
    Kenney DeCamp
Cuba AC/BC (After & Before Castro)
    Eladio Amores
The Other Europe
    Wojtek Sawa & Margot Zarzycka-Whitelaw

Eladio Amores providing a presentation about Cuba at the Selby Library

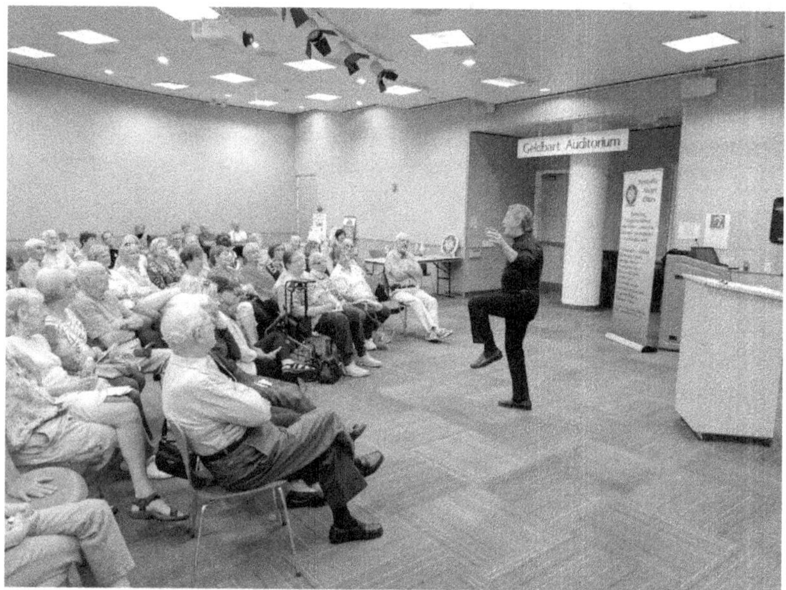

Kenney DeCamp illustrating Global Body Language

Sarasota Sister Cities Association Presentation
Madagascar and the Lemurs
Barbara Frey & Dr. Alison Grand

4:00 pm
March 9, 2017
Selby Library
1331 First Ave, Sarasota

History & Arts

History of the Israel Connection to Sarasota-Manatee
  Kim Sheintal
War & Peace
  Craig Hullinger, Beth Ruyle, Troy Scott & Ray Young
The Golden Age of Sarasota
  David Harralson, Ph.D.

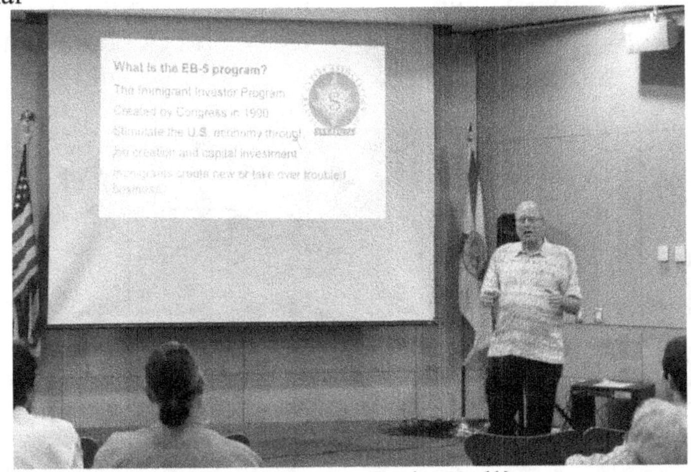

Science & Environment

City Sustainability Programs
  Craig Hullinger
Essential Oils & Perfumes of the World
  Raymond Young, Ph.D.
Madagascar and the Lemurs
  Barbara Frey & Alison Grand, Ph.D.
NASA Space Plant Biology
  Ed Rosenthal

VP-Economic Development Craig Hullinger presentation
on Immigrant Investor Program

SCAS "Happy Hour, Meet & Greet" Gatherings

Following the presentations at the Selby Library members of the audience gather at a local restaurant for a "Happy Hour" to continue the lively discussions as shown in photos below.

Gloria Grenier, Kathryn Young, and Happy Dunn

Gloria Grenier, Beth Ruyle, Lilianne Shealy-Shrock, Charles and in back Craig Hullinger

Werner Knoop, Craig Hullinger, Briana Knoop, Beth Ruyle-Hullinger, and Yulia Gaukham

Susan Moir, John Freeman, Carolyn Bloomer Tom Halbert & Gayle Maxey

Happy Hour in the time of Covid, Siesta Key Beach, Sarasota
Kathryn Young in front center, you guess the rest!

One World Award Program

"An ode to our common humanity: "One World – Out of Many, We are One."
Honoring Extraordinary People and Organizations

The One World Award is the Sarasota Sister Cities premier international award that honors one **Remarkable Individual** and one **Outstanding Organization** that has enhanced "Understanding and Respect" among citizens of the world through their extraordinary work or volunteer service.

This award shines a spotlight on individuals and organizations that have demonstrated their continued ability to create and maintain strong bonds of peace and understanding among the world's citizens through their extraordinary work and service to the community. The awards are presented to honorees at our annual Gala Dinner. The program was created and initiated by former SCAS President Bill Wallace.

Individual Award Laureates

2011 Robert Roskamp

Robert & Dianna Roscamp

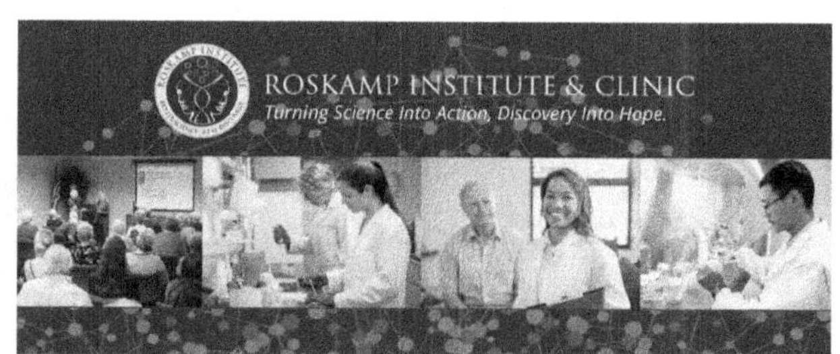

The Roskamp Institute is a worldwide leading institution in finding cures for Alzheimer's disease and mental disorders. The nonprofit biomedical research facility and neurology clinic specializes in elucidating the causes and treatments for neuropsychiatric and neurodegenerative diseases of Alzheimer's, traumatic brain injury and post-traumatic stress disorder.

2012 - Nicholas Bollettieri

Nick Bollettieri accepting OWA from SCAS President Tom Halbert

The IMG Nick Bollettieri Tennis Academy, became the IMG academy, and now is the world's largest and most advanced multi-sport training and educational institution. Bollettieri excelled in fostering international relationships that have impacted our Cultural Coast and individuals, families and communities around the world. He coached and developed gifted tennis players worldwide.

2013 - Former Mayor Lou Ann Palmer

Lou Ann Palmer was a public servant in Sarasota for 35 years serving as mayor five different times over three decades. She has served on the Board of Directors of Doctor's Hospital, Metropolitan Planning Organization, Key Rotary Club, Chamber of Commerce Leadership Program and as a Trustee of the Hospice of Southwest Florida. As mayor, she led the development of Sarasota and personally enhanced relationships with five Sarasota Sister Cities.

2014 – Linda Rosenbluth

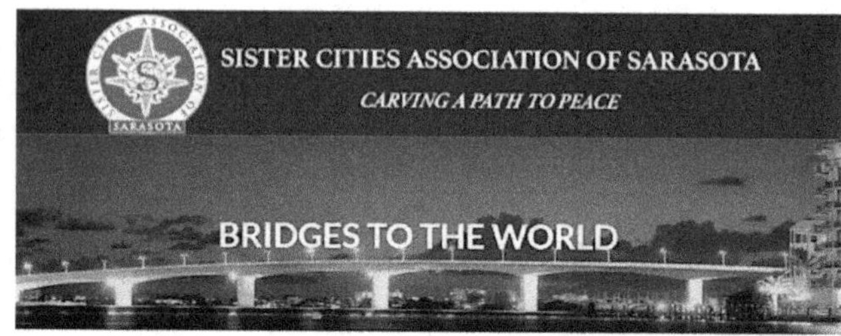

Former President & City Director for SCAS. Linda organized the first non-profit event at the Van Wezel Performing Arts Center in Sarasota, the first "phonathon" for United Way and Sarasota's first "AIDS Awareness Week", an initiative duplicated in communities nationwide. She has represented Sarasota on missions to Azerbaijan, Morocco, Poland and Israel, and enhanced relationships with officials and citizens of our sister cities.

2015 – Andrew Ezzell & JoAnn Patrick Ezzell

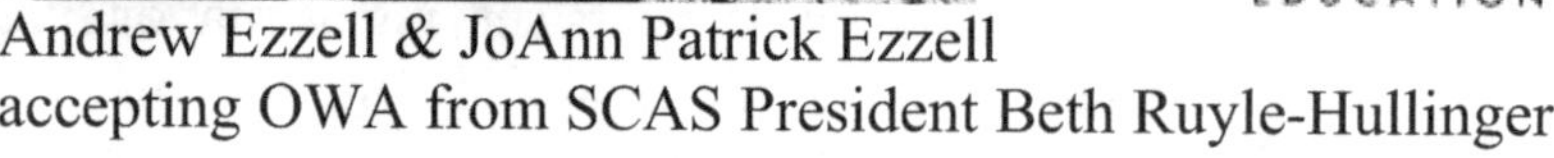

Andrew Ezzell & JoAnn Patrick Ezzell
accepting OWA from SCAS President Beth Ruyle-Hullinger

SCAS patron members, Andrew and JoAnn's Give Something Back Foundation has built Schools, Classrooms & Libraries in Vietnam, Thailand & Haiti, provided educational opportunities for Girls in Afghanistan and developed a Collaborative Online Education Program, including an international website competition for Students and Teachers around the World.

2016 – Dolly Jacobs and Pedro Reis

Dolly and Pedro combined their expertise and passion for the circus by creating Circus Sarasota which became the Circus Arts Conservatory. Their mission is to provide a circus that represents the circus arts at the highest level and that is linked to the community through performance, education and integrated arts programming. Eighty percent of ticket revenue is used for community outreach programs that serve children, the elderly and those in care facilities. The year-round outreach programs are Humor Therapy Program, an Education Program and Sailor Circus.

2017 – Dr. Mary Elmendorf

Mary Elmendorf receiving honorary
doctorate from Brown University

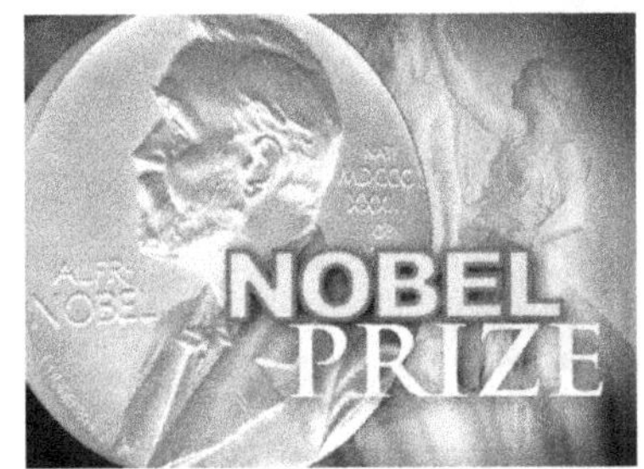

Dr. Elmendorf is an internationally known anthropologist and has been called the modern day Margaret Meade. She broke the glass ceiling for women by becoming the first woman director of the CARE program in Mexico, and is praised for translating anthropology into action. She gained international attention for her work with the Mayan women in Mexico. She was also the first anthropologist to work for the World Bank and a **Nobel Prize** winner for her work with Spanish refugees in France after WWII.

2018 – Kate Alexander

Actress, Associate Director and the founder of the Florida Studio Theater's Theatre School, Kate Alexander established the "Write-a-Play" program as an international component of the Young Playwrights Festival in which our international Sister Cities students participate.

2020 - Maestro Víctor DeRenzi

 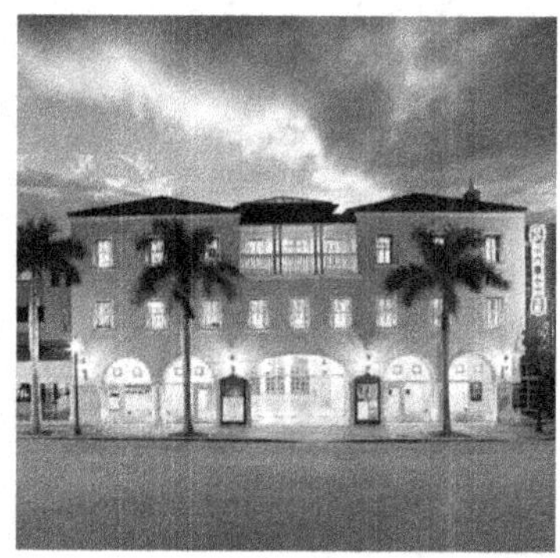

Maestro Víctor DeRenzi is Sarasota Opera's Principal Conductor and Artistic Director. Maestro DeRenzi is lauded for advancing world peace and understanding through exchanges in music and the performing arts as well as the historic completion of the Verdi Cycle. DeRenzi is the only conductor to have performed every piece of classical music composed by Maestro Giuseppi Verdi. This historic effort known as the "Verdi Cycle" took 28 years to accomplish together with the Sarasota Opera, and garnered Maestro DeRenzi international praise. Verdi's home of Busseto, is our newest Friendship City.

Organization Award Laureates

2012 - ORT America

Accepting the OWA trophy for ORT are (l to r), Gulfside Palm ORT Chapter
President Marlies Gluck, SaraMana ORT Chapter President Lynn Sacks and
National ORT President Shelley Fagel

ORT currently educates and develops career skills for many individuals in 55
countries. Although it is the largest Jewish educational institution in the world, it
educates both Jewish and non-Jewish children and adults. Since 1960, ORT has
been invited to sponsor humanitarian programs in more than 100 countries, tailoring
its curriculum to the needs of the student population in that country. ORT had its
beginnings in Tsarist Russia in 1880 and today has a focus on science and high-tech
in addition to its other multiple course offerings.

Students in ORT Summer Skills Program

At the One World Gala sponsored by Sister Cities Association of Sarasota. The
following was presented at the gala by SCAS President Bill Wallace:
*"How in this One World could one even imagine trying to organize a program to
educate 300,000 individuals annually across the globe. Just ask ORT – it seems
able to do anything – and it's been doing it for over 130 years! And that's why ORT
was the very first organization chosen to receive the prestigious One World Award
of the Sarasota Sister City Association."*

2013 – Sarasota Christian School

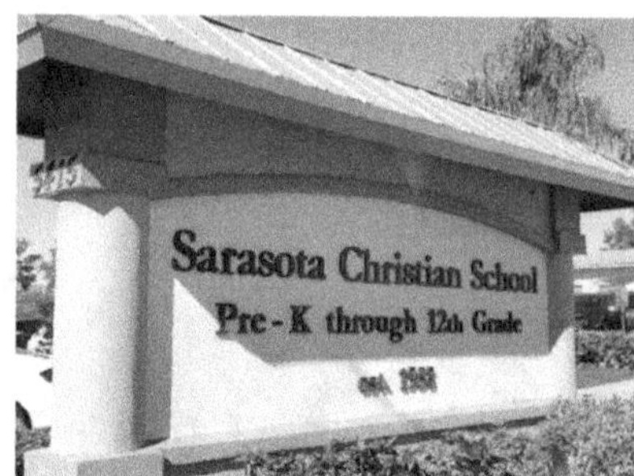

Jeff Shank & Dawn Graber accepting OWA on behalf of SCS

Sarasota Christian School has promoted diversity and international relationships and has supported and maintained connections with schools in twelve foreign countries. The school has an active international student body. The award was accepted by school representatives Jeffrey Shank and Dawn Graber.

2014 - Embracing Our Differences

Embracing Our Differences promotes a world where differences are embraced and individuality is celebrated. Art is a powerful tool to evoke social change. Artists can enlighten, educate and affect change around the world. The program employs art as a catalyst to spark discussions and promote the importance of peaceful coexistence achieved through a huge outdoor exhibit at Sarasota's City Island Park. The exhibit is viewed by hundreds of thousands of people each year and 90% indicated that it had favorably influenced their opinions regarding diversity and inclusion of people everywhere.

2015 - Sarasota Audubon Society

Jeanne Dubi, President
Sarasota Audubon Society

Nature Center at Celery Fields

Led by Sarasota Audubon President, Jeanne Dubi, a former 400 acre storm water reclamation site was turned into one of Florida's leading Wildlife Habitats for Local & Migratory Birds. Celery Fields offers paths, boardwalks and observation sites with native plants and wildlife. One and a quarter million dollars of private funds were raised to construct a Nature center at the site. Sarasota Audubon also has an extensive program for Instruction of both youth and adults including classes, workshops and field trips. Over 10,000 visitors, not only Sarasota, but also from all over the USA and around the world, partake in these programs each year.

2018 - Second Chance-Last Opportunity

Dr. April Glasco, President Second Chance-Last Opportunity

The mission of Second Chance-Last Opportunity is to empower people in crisis by providing them with essential skills and tools so they can manage their lives more productively. Founded by April Glasco, the current CEO, she was an owner of a store in the Newtown community that struggles with issues of crime, drugs, domestic violence, and unemployment. She closed her storefront, gave away its contents, and in 1995 re-opened the store as Second Chance-Last Opportunity, a hands-on intervention center.

2020 – The Sarasota Opera

Richard Russell (r), Director Sarasota Opera receiving OWA trophy from
City Manager Marlon Brown at SCAS OWA Gala

Under the leadership of Richard Russell and Victor DeRenzi Sarasota Opera is "Verdi's American Home," the only company in the world to have performed all of his works. The award recognizes the contribution the Sarasota Opera has made to the community through music education and appreciation in the performing arts. The City of Sarasota recognized this incredible distinction by naming the street in front of the Opera House – Verdi Place.

Sarasota Sister Cities Gala

Sarasota Sister Cities holds a Gala Dinner event once a year. This is a major social event and fundraiser. The Gala features entertainment and the awarding of our prestigious One World Award to the honorees, both individual and organizational.

Each Gala has a theme reflecting one of our sister cities as shown in the poster for the Treviso Gala in 2017.

Women all decked out for the Festa Gala

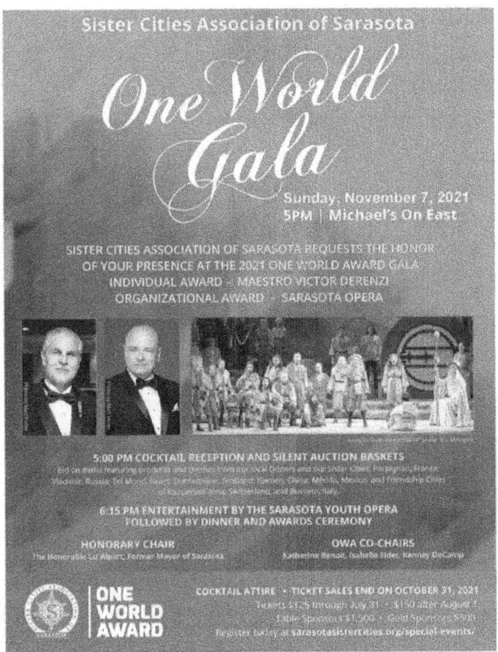

Gala poster honoring
Maestro Victor DeRenzi

Former mayors attending SCAS Gala
Mayors Susan Atwell, Lou Ann Palmer
and Marianne Servian

Embracing Our Differences Program

Embracing Our Differences mission is "to promote diversity and respect, not as an alternative to a sense of cultural and national identity, but as an essential part of life in the 21st century. The Sarasota Sister Cities Association works in cooperation with the Embracing Our Differences (EOD) program that promotes diversity in the world. We invite contributions of paintings and photos as well as quotes from our Sister City communities and friends, families and affiliates in Manatee and Sarasota counties to take part in the annual International Contest of "Embracing Our Difference". This contest is open to everyone regardless of location, age or occupation.

During April and May each year, Embracing Our Differences employs art as a catalyst to spark discussions and promote the importance of peaceful coexistence, creating a huge outdoor exhibit at Sarasota's Island Park, displaying the art of both national and international artists, photographers, writers and students.

Since its inception a decade ago, the exhibit has attracted thousands of submissions from 64 countries. In 2013, the exhibit drew over 4,400 international submissions representing 52 countries and was viewed by 248,000 visitors. Ninety percent indicated that the display favorably influenced their opinion regarding diversity and inclusiveness of people everywhere.

During the past several years, 20-25% of all artists selected for inclusion in the exhibit were international and in 2013, 18 artists from 14 foreign nations were honorees, including "Best of Show Adult" - an Israeli artist who had previously visited Sarasota with her family to see the display.

In responding to the announcement that Embracing Our Differences was to receive the SCAS One World Award, Michael Shelton, Executive Director of Embracing Our Differences said, "We're making a difference. The One World Award is a recognition of that. It's a formidable honor and we're deeply grateful."

Artists from four of Sarasota's eight sister cities: Dunfermline, Scotland; Vladimir, Russia; Tel Mond, Israel and Xiamen, China have had billboards at the EOD annual exhibit. The art exhibit is located at Bayfront Park adjacent to the Sarasota Sister Cities Tree Walk and is held from January 20 through April 1. Further information about the program is available on their website: embracing our differences.org.

Florida Sister Cities State Convention

SCAS hosted the Florida Sister Cities State Convention in 2005 and in May, 2013 at the Helmsley Sandcastle Resort on Lido Key in Sarasota. The occasion also marked the 50th anniversary of the founding of SCAS. The event featured speakers from SCAS, Sarasota City leaders and with a special keynote presentation by Sister Cities International President & CEO Mary Kane. Former Mayor Lou Ann Palmer provided a personal and passionate presentation on her many years of involment with Sarasota Sister Cities. A series of interactive discussions were also held as part of the event.

Sarasota Mayor Susan Atwell, SCI President & CEO Mary Kane and SCAS President Tom Halbert at the Convention

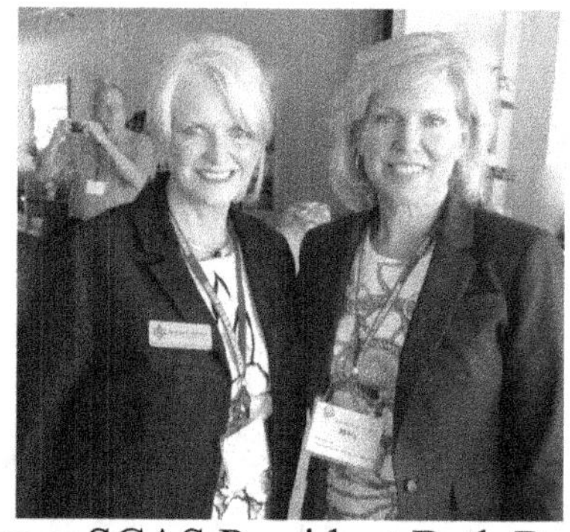

Former SCAS President Beth Ruyle and SCI President Mary Kane

Soprano and Former SCAS President Hope Byrnes singing "Let There Be Peace on Earth" at the Convention after presentation by former Sarasota Mayor Lou Ann Palmer on right.

Ray Young, SCAS VP-Education led an Interactive discussion on "Youth and Education Innovation"

Festival-4-Life

SCAS participated in the Dakin Dairy Farms "Festival-4-Life" at their location in Myakka, Florida. Our association offered an international tasting competition between all of our sister cities, with food provided by Sarasota restaurants. Kenney DeCamp obtained the commitments from the Sarasota restaurants and organized the tasting event. The following list shows the sister city, the sponsoring restaurant and the sister city member hosting each tasting booth.
Dunfermline – MacAllisters (Pauline Mitchell),
Treviso – Café Gabbiano (Kenney DeCamp),
Tel Mond – Louies Modern (Ray Young),
Perpignan – C'est La Vie (Gloria Grenier),
Vladimir – Russian House (Yuliya Gaukman),
Xiamen – Yummy House (Irene Leung),
Hamilton – Morton's (Dave Harrelson,
Merida - Pablano's Mexican Restaurant (Mike Fehily).

SCAS Sponsored Community Trolley Tours

Several local educational trolley tours have been arranged by SCAS for the community and SCAS members. The sightseeing tours provide a history of various aspects of Sarasota. Some of the tours focus on a particular community in Sarasota, for example, the history of the African American community of Newtown in Sarasota and the Amish community in Sarasota.

Participants in an SCAS sponsored trolley tour of Sarasota

Promotional Events

An annual SCAS promotional event is held to educate the community about our activities and to enhance our membership. Often a table or booth is set up with our brochures containing information about SCAS and membership application forms. The contents of the promotional brochure are shown in the section on Brochures.

Kenney DeCamp & Christine Rufino and Alice Cotman on right with a display of SCAS materials for promotion of SCAS at Sarasota Chamber of
Commerce community event

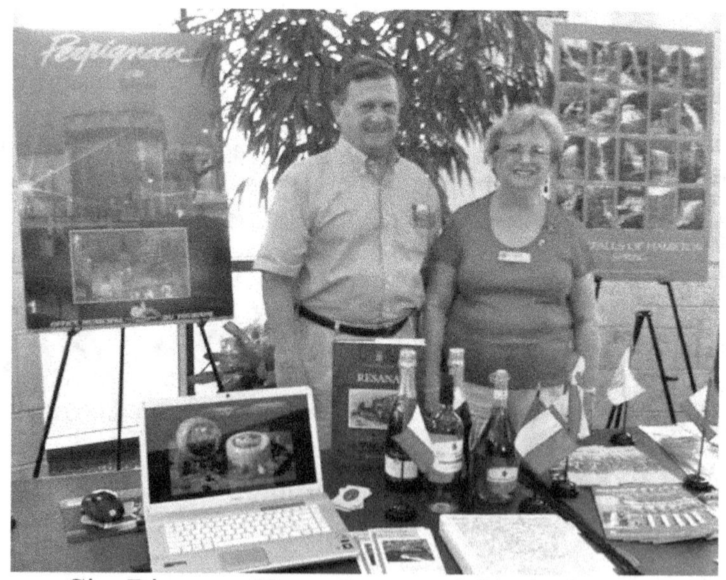

Former Perpignan City Directors Harry Dunn and Gloria Grenier with display of
pictures and items from Perpignan

President Miriam Kramer presenting
overview of SCAS

City Director Ivonne Henry describing
special feature of Perpignan

Presentations at the SCAS Showcase Promotional Event at USF Nov 14, 2023

Grisell Aleman & Mike Fehily describing special features of Merida

Asst City Director Dennis Ciborowski describing home of Verdi in Busseto

Presentations at the SCAS Showcase Promotional Event at USF Nov 14, 2023

Linda Rosenbluth, Kim Sheintal & Rabbi Jonathan Katz at Tel Mond Booth

Pauline Mitchell offering libations at Dunfermline booth

Promotional booths at the SCAS Showcase Promotional Event
at USF Nov 14, 2023

In front of Xiamen booth at SCAS Showcase Promotional Event at USF Nov 14, 2023 (l to r) Jill Dye, ACD Duane Finger, City Director **Kun Shi,** **ACD Larry Bennison and Former President Miriam Kramer**

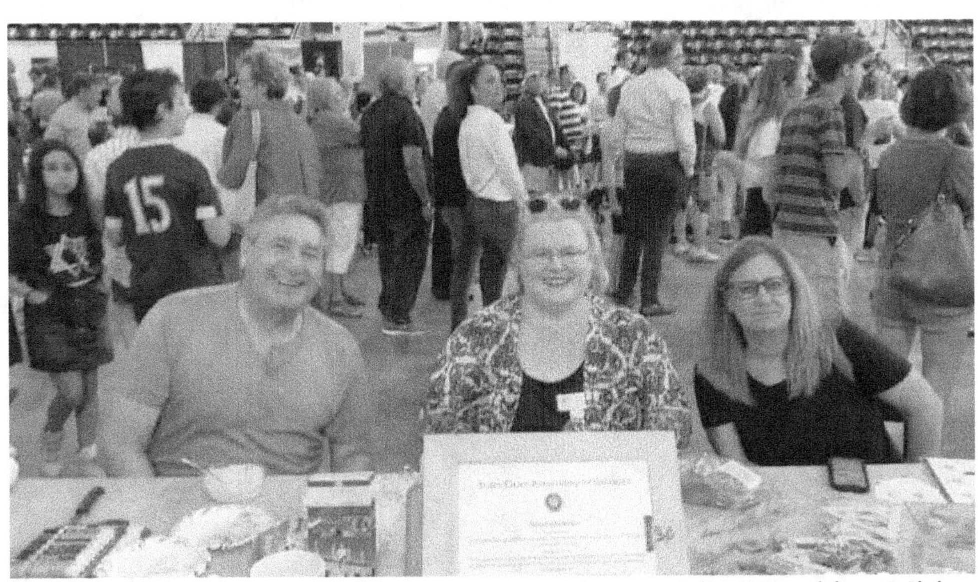

Former City Director Rabbi Jonathan Katz, Former SCAS President Miriam Kramer and incoming new SCAS President Diana Foreman Freeman at SCAS promotional table for 75th anniversary of Israel with the Jewish Federation

Awards and Honors Bestowed on SCAS

SCAS has received numerous awards and honors for accomplishment in our mission of promoting peace and understanding in the world.

The awards are listed below and include:

1968 – Special **"People-to-People Award"** for numerous exchanges with the first sister city, Santo Domingo. Bestowed by Sister Cities International.

2002 – **"Best Overall Program Award"** for involving many sister cities in our joint programs. From Sister Cities International.

2010. – **"Sustainability Award"** for the student exchange program with Perpignan focused on Solar Energy. From the U.S. Department of Energy ($1,000)

2010 - **"Innovation Award: Sustainability"** for the student exchange program with Perpignan focused on Solar Energy. From Sister Cities International.

2015 – **"Innovation Award: Arts & Culture" for the Write-a-Play Competition** in cooperation with the Florida Studio Theater. From Sister Cities International.

<u>Movers and Shakers – Making it all happen</u> (l to rt), Former SCAS President Miriam Kramer, VP-Arts & Culture Sue Gordon, CD-Dunfermline, Pauline Mitchell and former President & City Director-Tel Mond Linda Rosenbluth

Sister City Signage and Memorials

Sarasota Sister Cities is represented throughout the city with signage and memorials at numerous locations. The "Welcome to Sarasota" signs are on highways leading into the city and identify our Sister Cities. The one shown below is on Fruitville Road on the westbound side just before Cardinal Mooney High School.

Welcome Sister City Sign on route to Sarasota

We are also represented on Sarasota's Bayfront Island with several descriptive plaques and signs that include our mission of peace and understanding in the world and a list of our sister cities. Our **Sister Cities Tree Walk** has a tree dedicated to each of our sister cities with a sign providing the date of acceptance by our city government. Bayfront Island and Park is located in downtown Sarasota near O'Leary's Tiki Bar. For 15 years Vice President Ray Young ensured that the signs were well maintained and replaced when necessary.

Sister City Tree Walk on Sarasota Bayfront

Linda Rosenbluth working hard to plant tree commemorating
Sister City Tel Mond, Israel

Xiamen delegation viewing plaque for tree planted for their city in the Tree Walk

Xiamen Tree Plaque

Sister Cities Official Office

The City of Sarasota provides very nice office space for Sarasota Sister Cities. We are located on the first floor of the historic Federal Building at 111 South Orange Avenue. It was originally constructed in 1931 in a Neoclassical Revival Style as a Post Office. The building was described as a "Classical design of the Corinthian type, fireproofed throughout with steel structure piling in the foundations. One radical innovation in the then new Post Office was the use of marble and aluminum where metal was ordinarily employed in parts of the building used by the public."

Federal Building in Sarasota

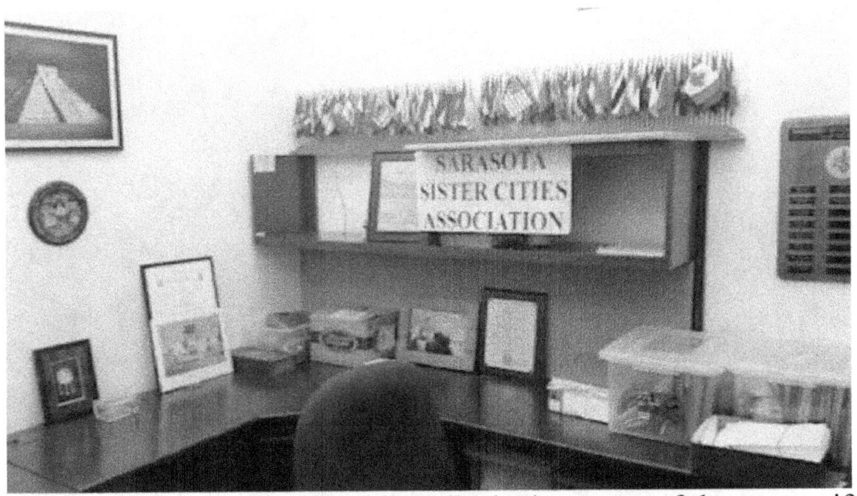

SCAS Office in Federal Building displaying some of the many gifts from our Sister Cities

Sister Cities Sustainability Conference Brochure

Below is the promotional brochure distributed for the SCAS Sustainability Conference described in a previous section. It shows both the breadth and depth of the presentations in the symposium that was held at the University of South Florida-Sarasota/Manatee.

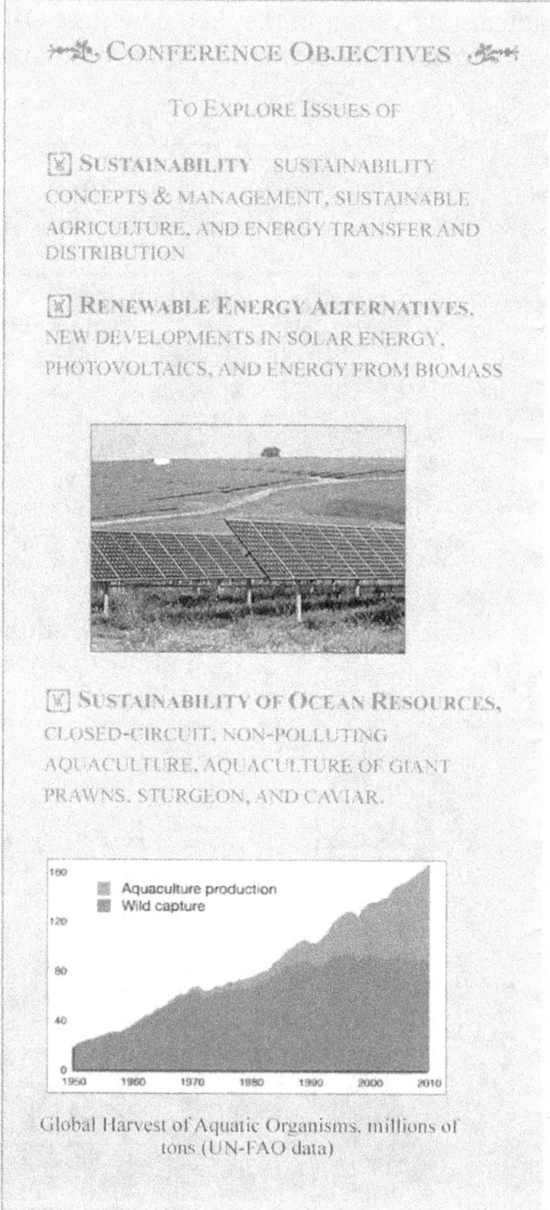

Global Harvest of Aquatic Organisms, millions of tons (UN-FAO data)

Sister Cities Association of Sarasota

One of the major missions of Sister Cities Association of Sarasota (SCAS) is to foster international relationships between Sarasota and its sister cities through exchanges in areas of culture and education. SCAS's objective is to develop respect, understanding and cooperation through citizen diplomacy. In furtherance of this objective. SCAS is planning a three day conference on *"Sustainability Through Renewable Energy and Aquaculture"* for November 13-15, 2013 at the University of South Florida – Sarasota/Manatee . The goal of the conference is to bring together both professionals and students from institutions located in our Sister Cities and Sarasota area institutions in a forum based on Sustainability.

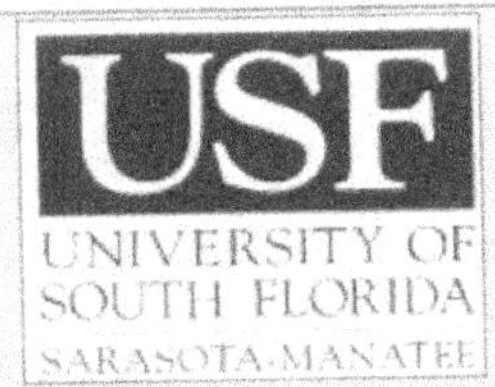

PRESENTERS & PARTICIPANTS

The topics for the conference will emphasize expertise in the Sarasota area as well as in our Sister Cities. A special student session is planned were local and sister city college and high school students will have the opportunity to interact through both poster and summary oral presentations.

Regional presentations are planned from the University of South Florida, State College of Florida, Ringling College of Arts & Design, New College of Florida and University of Florida-Extension in the areas of Sustainability; from the University of Central Florida, Solar Energy Center and the U.S. Dept. of Agriculture in the area of Renewable Energy and from Mote Marine Laboratories and the National Oceanographic and Atmospheric Administration in Aquaculture. This will be complimented by Sister City presentations in these topic areas from University of Perpignan, **Perpignan**, France; Carnegie College, **Dunfermline**, Scotland; Autonomous University of the Yucatan, **Merida**, Mexico; Interdisciplinary Center, **Tel Mond**, Israel; University of Padua, **Treviso**, Italy and Jimei University, **Xiamen**, China. It is planned that a professional speaker from each of the sister city institutions will be accompanied by several college and/or high school students for participation in the conference.

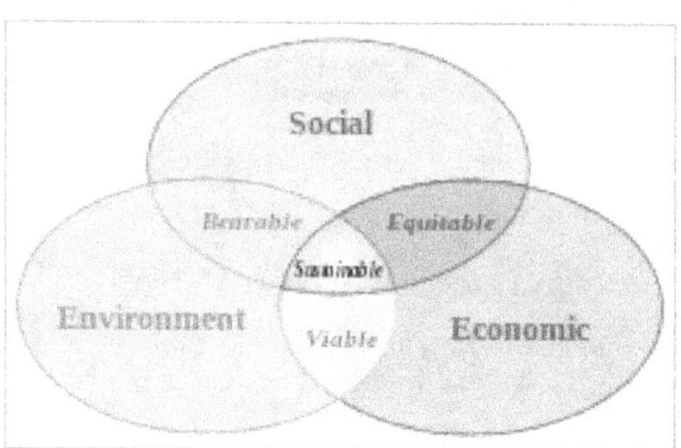

Sustainability creates and maintains the conditions for humans and nature to live in harmony and meet the needs of present and future generations. It is the confluence of Social, Economic and Environmental constituents. Major progressive corporations have embraced the concept and practices of sustainability not only for financial gain but for the benefit of communities, cities and governments.

Additional Information Contact:
Dr. Raymond A. Young
aloharay4@gmail.com

Sarasota is situated on the Gulf Coast of Florida, often referred to as the cultural coast. The city enjoys 330 days of sunshine per year and is a popular tourist destination. The beaches are some of the best in the world with Siesta Key beach rated number one due to its pearly white sand of 99% quartz. The city boasts the world renowned Ringling Museum containing European and contemporary art as well as an extensive Circus Museum. Mote Marine Laboratories on Lido Key houses an aquarium, sea animal rescue facilities and an extensive marine research program. Sarasota provides and excellent venue for a Sustainability Conference.

Sister Cities Promotional Brochure

The most recent SCAS promotional brochure was composed by a committee led by VP-Membership David Harralson as shown below.

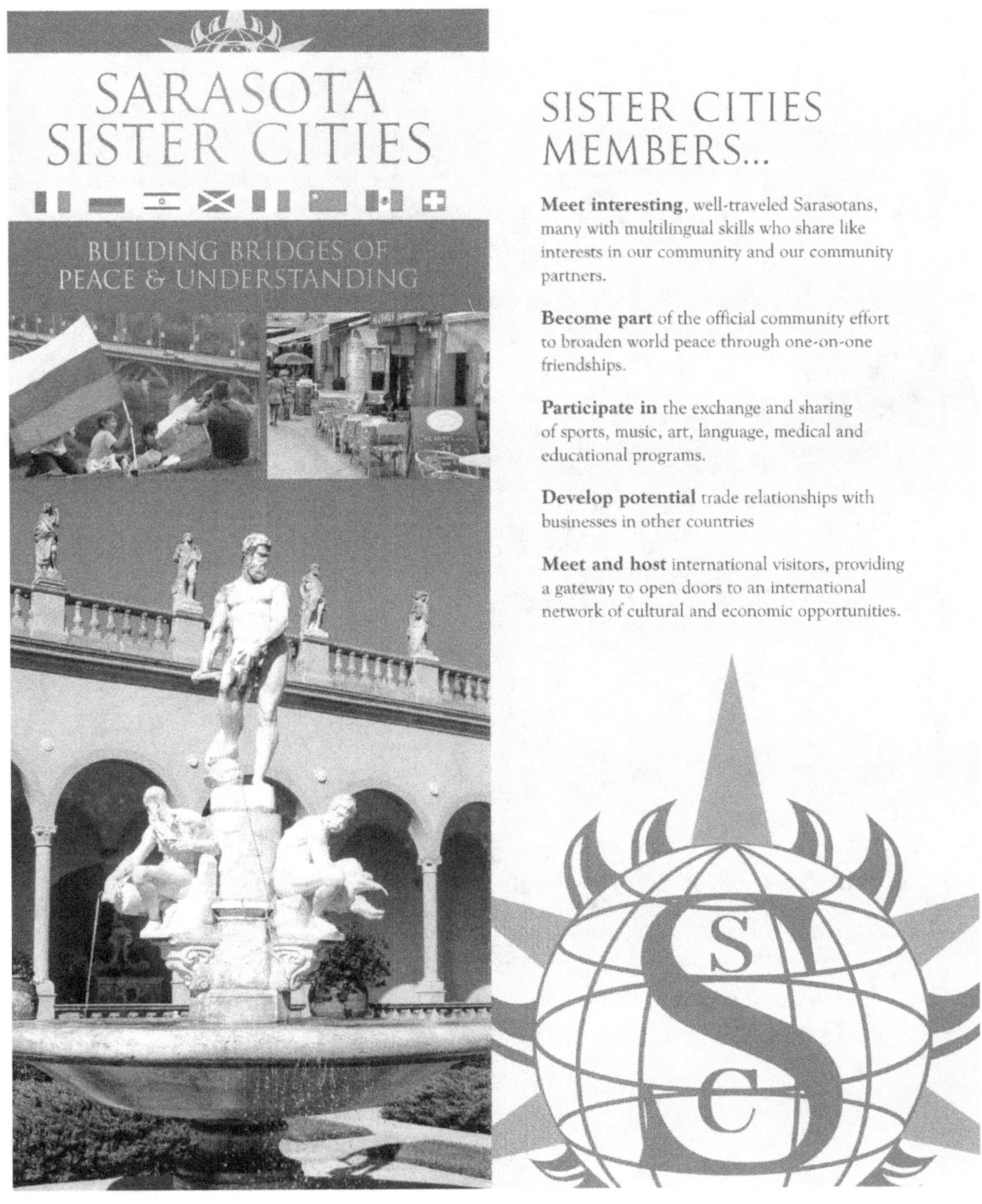

GOALS & MISSION

The Sister Cities' objective is to develop respect, understanding and cooperation through citizen diplomacy.

Sister Cities fosters international relationships between Sarasota and cities with similar interests. Working outside the realm of government, but with its support, we encourage and facilitate cultural and educational exchanges, business opportunities and increased tourism.

EVENTS & PROJECTS

CULTURAL
Music, art, film, dance, and other exchanges between sister cities.

ECONOMIC
Forming alliances with economic development organizations to foster international business through professional and technical exchanges.

EDUCATION
Scholarships, student visits, and book and equipment donations to schools and libraries in our sister cities.

DIGITAL
Internet exchanges of art, student projects and penpal with our communications sister cities.

DIPLOMATIC
Citizen Diplomats explore other cultures through long-term partnerships.

LUNCHEONS & EVENTS
From September–May, luncheons and evening events focus on our sister cities and community events of interest to members.

MUNICIPAL
Exchanges of resources, information and ideas among municipal and regional government officials.

SPORTS & YOUTH
Hosting and facilitating visits by sports teams and youth organizations to and from our sister cities.

OUR SISTER CITIES

HAMILTON, ONTARIO, CANADA 1990 Hamilton boasts a diversity that combines education, culture and sightseeing attractions with business and commerce, especially steel manufacturing.

PERPIGNAN, FRANCE 1994 A cultural business, university town and business center situated just west of the Mediterranean Sea, surrounded by the Pyrenees Mountains and beautiful vineyards, and is known for its excellent wines.

VLADIMIR, RUSSIA 1994 A historical city dating back to the 1100's with today's focus on the development of tourist attractions, while maintaining an impressive focus on the arts and education.

TEL MOND, ISRAEL 1999 Located just north of Tel Aviv, Tel Mond, like Sarasota, is situated in the midst of orange groves and productive farmland. With an emphasis on its youth and education, the city is expanding its educational campus.

DUNFERMLINE, SCOTLAND 2002 Once the ancient capital of Scotland under Malcolm III, Dunfermline is the final resting place of King Robert the Bruce and is the birthplace of philanthropist Andrew Carnegie. Dunfermline is becoming home for contemporary business opportunities and cultural activities providing links between our two cities.

TREVISO, ITALY 2007 Replete with the amenities of the 21st century, Treviso is situated within beautifully preserved renaissance settings just northwest of Venice and the Adriatic. It is noted for cultural, historical, gastronomical, manufacturing, agricultural, and ecological highlights.

XIAMEN (SIMING DISTRICT), CHINA 2006 A port on China's southeast coast, China's 5th most environmentally clean city, and 2004 winner of the UN Habitat Award. Among the most sought-after places to live in China, this modern city is home to a national key university, an international airport, historic Gulangyu Island, a spectacular botanical garden, a 1400-year old working Buddhist temple, and much more.

MÉRIDA, MEXICO 2010 The vibrant capital of the Mexican state of Yucatán has a rich Mayan and colonial heritage. Located close to the tip of the Yucatán, it has long been called "the white city" because of its many buildings built of white limestone. Its Mayan-inspired cuisine sets it apart from the rest of Mexico.

RAPPERSWIL-JONA, SWITZERLAND (Friendship City) 2015 Known as the Town of Roses, it is located on the upper end of Lake Zurich. Combining scenic vistas, cultural life, hiking and sports with a Mediterranean holiday atmosphere, it is often called the Riviera of Lake Zurich.

CITIZEN DIPLOMACY
THE SISTER CITIES STORY

In 1956, President Dwight D. Eisenhower proposed a people-to-people program under the National League of Cities as one of *citizen diplomacy*. He envisaged persons and organizations in individual U.S. cities interacting on a one-to-one basis with piers in foreign cities, believing that such personal relationships would lessen future world conficts.

The program grew rapidly and became the nonprofit Sister Cities International in 1967. Even before, in 1963, Sarasota had already established the Sister Cities Association of Sarasota.

Sister City Business Brochure

A committee was formed of local business people and SCAS representatives including Gloria Grenier and Raymond Young. The brochure was developed to highlight the special opportunities of doing business in Sarasota. It was a way for SCAS to further contribute to our community by attracting international investors. The brochure is shown below and the last page of the brochure is an example of a targeted approach to one of our sister cities, in this case for Perpignan, France.

SISTER CITIES ASSOCIATION OF SARASOTA

DOING BUSINESS WITH SARASOTA, FLORIDA

Sister Cities International is a nonprofit network that creates and strengthens partnerships among communities around the world. In the United States, more than 522 cities are partnered with 2012 communities in 143 countries. The Sister Cities organization aims to build global cooperation at the municipal level, promote cultural understanding and stimulate economic development. This document summarizes _why Doing Business in Sarasota_ is mutually advantageous to our societies and _how easy_ it is to initiate the process.

Why Do Business in Florida?

The United States of America is known as favorable to the free enterprise/competitive market system with few barriers to entry and a stable regulatory environment. Florida is a fast growing, prosperous and pro-business state which actively pursues the expansion of existing business, relocation of businesses and creation of new businesses.

The factors which distinguish Florida from other US states are:

- Florida is the only US state on the east coast with no state personal income tax
- In 2014, Florida was the number 2 US state in terms of technical job creation
- Given the climate, style of life and no income tax, Florida has the second highest population growth of all the US states
- Situated on the Atlantic Ocean and Gulf of Mexico, Florida has excellent air, water, railroad and road links to the entire continental US and is the major transportation "hub" to the Caribbean and South America. Florida has the second largest Free Trade Zone network in the US
- Florida ranks number 5 of all US states in terms of employment by enterprises with a majority of foreign ownership
- 80 countries have a Consular Corps representation in

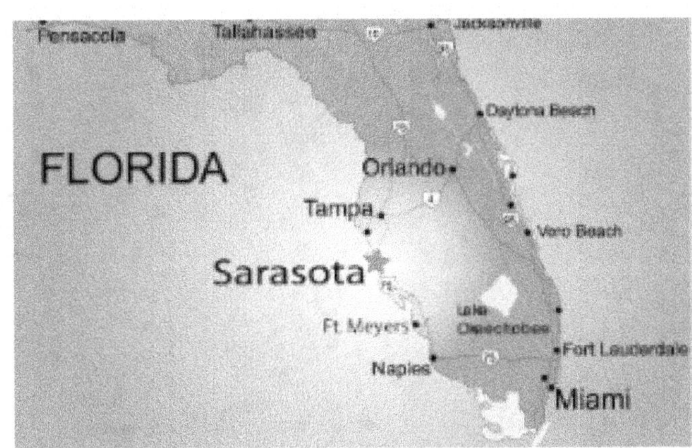

The State of Florida actively supports two organizations specifically designed to promote business development. The Enterprise Florida, Inc. (EFI) is a public-private initiative to stimulate the economy via job creation: (www.enterpriseflorida.com). GrowFL is a program dedicated to assist enterprise owners/CEOs of companies with 10 to 99 employees (or $1-50 million in revenues) identify core business strategies and implementation plans (www.GrowFL.com).

Why Do Business in Sarasota, Florida?

If Florida meets your business needs, Sarasota will exceed your dreams of a place for you and your family to live and enjoy the beaches, climate, sports, theatre, arts, museums, restaurants, educational opportunities, travel. Business promotion is a high priority for greater Sarasota and in 2009 the local governments and civic organizations created the Economic Development Corporation of Sarasota County (EDC). The EDC published a basic reference document for prospective business clients and interested civic organizations: Sarasota County, Florida Profile: Locate Your Business Where You Want to Live! (Herein identified as "Profile") This guide is available in hard copy or on-line at www.edcsarasotacounty.com. The major economic incentives and fiscal benefits identified by the Profile for creation,

relocation, or augmentation of business in the greater Sarasota area are summarized below:

Economic environment and infrastructure:

- Sarasota-Bradenton-North Port area ranks second in the largest metro areas in the US for economic performance (Brookings Institute 2012),
- Port of Tampa and Port of Manatee and International Airports in Tampa, Sarasota/Bradenton, St. Petersburg-Clearwater and Fort Myers are all within 90 minute drive from Sarasota
- Business Parks, Special Energy Economic Zones and small business HUB Zones offer a cafeteria of choices for business site selection,

Sarasota Bay

- Florida Power & Light, Peoples Gas and Sarasota County Utilities are all highly competitive and offer a series of environmental rebates

Financing Incentives

- Economic Development Incentive Grants

- Capital Investment Tax Credits
- Performance Incentive Grants for selected sectors
- Enterprise and Industrial Revenue Bonds
- Small Business Administration Loans

The major partners engaged in *Doing Business with Sarasota* are the Sarasota County Office of Business and Economic Development, the Chamber of Commerce of Greater Sarasota, and the Economic Development Corporation of Sarasota with the Sister Cities Association of Sarasota providing outreach and coordination with our international sister city partners and businesses.

Sarasota is open for business!
To initiate *Doing Business with Sarasota*, the Sister Cities Association of Sarasota invites you to contact us at: sarasotasistercities @gmail.com

Solar Energy Array

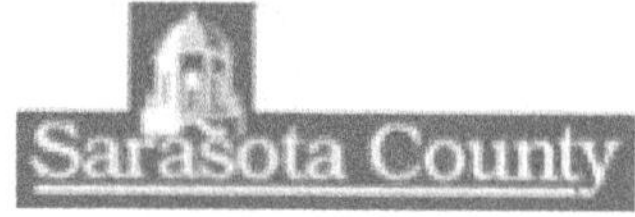

The Linkages between Sarasota and Perpignan

The greater Sarasota area is approximately the same size, in both land mass and size of population, compared to its sister-city Perpignan and the Pyrenees-Orientales Department of France. Moreover, the twinned areas of Sarasota and Perpignan share in common many attributes and characteristics. Vacation resorts, host salt-water aquatic industries (fisheries, research in marine biology and water sports) and have developed long-range plans for centers of expertise in technological research and business development.

The Economic Development Corporation of Sarasota and the Agence de Développement Economique (Agency for Economic Development) of the Perpignan Metropolitan Area are perfect partners to stimulate, assist (with finance and technical assistance) and mentor business exchanges between our countries. An early priority for the *Doing Business with Sarasota* is an exchange of information and activities by these two agencies, based on this document and the " Perpignan Méditerranée, A Territory of Excellence," prepared by the Agence in France. The 2014-2015 plan of action of the Sarasota Sister Cities Association envisages a visit by a delegation from Perpignan to Sarasota in 2015, to include, hopefully, the Mayor of Perpignan, members of the Sister Cities of Perpignan, the Director of the Agence de Développement Economique and business persons from Perpignan.

According to Le Journal Français Des Etats-Unis (Actualités 2 October 2014), some 3,000 French live within the west coast of Florida and more than 50 French companies are engaged in production and commerce, many of which are amongst the largest enterprises in France (Axa, Veolia, Bic, Sodexho, Safran). Indeed, France is the 4th largest source of investment in the region! French investors appear to seek two types of business opportunities in Florida:

First, manufacturers such as Monin (a large French gourmet flavoring products firm), use local natural resources (vegetables, fruits and sugar cane) in the production of their commodities for the US market and export to the Americas.

Second, some other French companies employ their own/ proprietary technology to the US market; for example, Veolia provides water treatment in the region and Saint-Gobain produces and sells their construction materials ("Placoplatre"). And, of course, technological innovations- be they from large companies or micro-enterprises- are the wave of the future.

Sister Cities and Sarasota partners (City of Sarasota, Sarasota County, Chamber of Commerce of Greater Sarasota, and Economic Development Corporation of Sarasota) are ready to assist you to find a local business associate/partner and/or to utilize the resources available to initiate an enterprise here. In addition, Sister Cities' French business colleagues can utilize the organizational and technical resources of the Alliance Française de Sarasota and the French and American Business Council of West Florida (FRAMCO) both of which are very active in the greater Sarasota area. So begin today, contact Sister Cities at: sarasotasistercities @gmail.com

Biographies of Some Former
SCAS Presidents & Board Members
(partial list)

Listed below are sample biographies of the background and the contributions to SCAS from some of the many volunteer members that have served on the Board of Directors of SCAS. The biographies demonstrate the expertise and broad dimension of the people that serve Sarasota Sister Cities. Most have served SCAS in the past years.

President Hope Byrnes

Hope Byrnes was President of Sister cities for seven years and restarted the Association with the help of City of Sarasota leaders. She was the first to report SCAS projects monthly at City government meetings. She visited most of our cities, and hosted visits to and from several of our cities. Hope spent her career in Washington, D.C. on Capitol Hill and later as the wife of a US Foreign Service Officer. She is a supurb soprano singer and performed at a major theater in Xiamen when the SCAS signing delegation visited Xiamen. She was President of several other organizations in Sarasota including the Sarasota Opera Guild and the Asolo Theatre Guild.

President Linda Rosenbluth

Former President and City Director for Tel Mond. Linda organized the first non-profit event at the Van Wezel Performing Arts Center in Sarasota, the first "Phonathon" for United Way and Sarasota's first "AIDS Awareness Week", an initiative duplicated in communities nationwide. She has represented Sarasota on missions to Azerbaijan, Morocco, Poland and Israel, and enhanced relationships with officials and citizens of our sister cities. Linda is an educator – a reading specialist and political science teacher- as well as a fun loving artist.

President Bill Wallace

Bill's career was in the financial services industry and he worked tirelessly to raise funds for SCAS over his many years of service. Bill initiated the SCAS "One World Award" and fund-raising Galas. He also served on the boards of many Sarasota organizations including, the Chamber of Commerce, New College Foundation, American Red Cross, Mental Health Community Centers and the Scottish Heritage Society. Bill co-founded and served as president of the Caledonian Club of Florida West. His BA is from Drake Univ. and he received the "Drake Alumni Loyalty Award." He also received the Rotary "Service Above Self Award" and the "Congressional Tartan Day Award." He wears his Scottish Kilt proudly.

President Carla Rayman Kidd
Carla was the President of Sister Cities and led the signing of Sister Cities
agreements with Xiamen, China and Merida, Mexico. She is a realtor with
Coldwell Banker of Sarasota and was the 2016-2020 National Association of
Realtors ® Global Coordinator to North America, Central America, & the
Caribbean. Carla was also chosen as realtor of the year in Sarasota. She is a noted
international instructor and speaker.

President Tom Halbert
Tom was the President of Sister Cities and guided the organization through difficult
times, rebuilding our finances. He also led the development of our website. Tom
started his career as a Newspaper and Service Reporter. He then became a combat
jet pilot in the Korean War followed by work with the Air Force Public Affairs
Program. He then had a 10 yr tenure as the executive manager of the Armed Forces
Radio & Television Europe. Tom holds a BA from Drake Univ. and an MA in
Public Relations from American Univ.

President Beth Ruyle
Beth led Sister Cities as President for four years. She was the former Director of the
South Suburban Mayors and Managers Association in Chicago and an Economic
Development Consultant with Ehlers Inc. She also worked for the Atlanta Regional
Commission. She has a BA from the University of Florida and an MA in
Government from the University of Georgia.

President Marianna Janz-Wecke
Mariana served as President from 2016 until her untimely death in 2018. She
worked with the German American Club and the Swiss-American Club in
supporting the development of the Friendship City Rappersville-Jona, Switzerland.
Previously Marianna was an elected member of the City Council in Germany and a
retail business owner. She worked as a realtor and was a community leader in
Sarasota.

President Toni Duval
Toni joined SCAS and served as the VP Communication in 2017 prior to becoming
the SCAS President from 2018 to 2020. She moved to the Sarasota area in 2016
from Knoxville, TN where she owned TLD-Training and Leadership Development
Enterprise. The business was a full-service employee development consulting firm.

President Miriam Kramer
Miriam currently serves as City Director for Vladimir. She has worked in
communications for non-profits in the fields of international media and
peacebuilding. She served as Director of Communications and Development for the
Alliance for Peacebuilding and as an editor for an international affairs quarterly.
Miriam has an MA in International Studies and Diplomacy from SOAS, Univ. of
London; and a BA in English Literature and Russian Language/Area Studies from
the College of William and Mary. She also studied in St. Petersburg and lived and

worked in Moscow. While serving as president she was awarded the Kathryn Davis Fellowship for Peace at Middlebury College

President Diana Forman-Friedman
Diana became president in 2023. She has served on many boards and committees for both local and international organizations including Friendship Force and Toastmasters. She has worked toward promoting peace by serving with the Girl Scouts of Southwest Florida, Meals on Wheels and SaraMana ORT. Diana has also hosted over 20 students and adults from 8 different countries. She is the co-owner of Ace Electric, Inc.

Treasurer Gloria Grenier
Gloria Grenier also served as Vice President of Arts and Culture for Sarasota Sister Cities. She has traveled widely, lived and worked in Paris for ten years and was in several the leadership positions of SCAS for over 15 years.

VP of Cities and Candidate Cities David Harralson
Dr. David Harralson volunteered for SCAS for many years and also at Mote Marine Laboratories. He published our newsletter during his time with SCAS. David was an English Professor and Administrator at Utica College/Syracuse Univ. and later became Director of the Library at the college. He directed tours to London and China for 25 years and offered his expertise for an SCAS trip to Merida. His BA is from Georgetown Univ., MA Indiana Univ., M.Ed. Syracuse Univ. and PhD from Kent State Univ.

Vice President Membership Isabelle Eidet
Isabelle Eidet was based in Washington, DC and worked for the Department of State for many years and has lived and worked in Italy, France, Switzerland, Austria, Philippines, Indonesia, Kenya, and India. Isabelle has considerable experience having served as President & Vice President on many NGO Boards in the US and overseas. She has been on the SCAS BOD since 2016 in various positions and helped design and launch our new website in 2019.

Vice President Arts and Culture Sue Gordon
Dr. Sue Gordon is a professor emeritus from Fielding Graduate University and past principal of the Center for Informed Practice, Policy and Research in Beverly, MA. In Sarasota she was a volunteer tutor for GED and ESL students. She holds an MA from Hunter College and a PhD in Sociology from the Univ. of Chicago.

Vice President Communications Jana Stanley
Jana is originally from Malaysia and was a teacher of Mandarin as a foreign language to students K-12 in international schools, both in the US and abroad. She has a BA in Chinese and MEd in Early Childhood Education. She loves to travel and enjoys learning about different cultures.

Vice President Education Dawn Graber
Dawn was employed for many years as an administrator at the Sarasota Christian
School. She has over 30 years of leadership and learning experience in multicultural
settings and had special involvement with international students program at SCS.
She is now a Senior Consultant with the Design Group International. She has a B.S.
from Goshen College and an M.A. from Eastern Mennonite Univ.

Vice President of Cities and City Director Tel Mond Rabbi Jonathan Katz
Jonathan served as a Rabbi at four different temples in the US. He was also the
Community Chaplain for the Jewish Federation of Sarasota-Manatee, leading the
Jewish Healing Program. Jonathan studied in Israel, Luxembourg and Paris and he
received a BA in arts from Miami Univ. and an MA in Hebrew letters from Hebrew
Union College.

Director of Events Charlotte Hull
Charlotte creatively organized our events ensuring interesting locations and
programs. She also served as the Assistant City Director for Rapperswil-Jona and
knows the community well. Charlotte formerly lived in Rapperswil-Jona where she
operated a successful hotel and restaurant business before moving to Sarasota.

City Director Busseto Phillip Gordon
Phillip is a native of Australia and prior to moving to the U.S. he lived many years
in both Italy and Switzerland. His career was in the travel industry as the CEO and
Chairman of Globus N.A.

City Director of Dunfermline Pauline Mitchell
Pauline's international life started in Indonesia where she was born. Educated in
The Netherlands and Switzerland, her career took her to Spain, Portugal and
Australia. Her deep interests lie in Scotland, a country she frequently traveled to
and has contributed many years as Dunfermline City Director. Her numerous trips
to Dunfermline have resulted in outstanding relations and lifelong friendships with
our Sister City.

City Director Merida Grisell Aleman
Grisell is originally from Mexico City but she moved to Merida when she was 13
years old and lived there for 16 years. She is a graphic designer and product
photographer. Grisell has worked tirelessly promoting exchanges with Merida.

City Director Perpignan Marie des Neiges Grossas
Dr. Marie des Neiges Grossas is a resident of both Sarasota and our Sister City
Perpignan, which gives her a unique perspective. She maintained contacts with
Perpignan for many years and arranged a special individual delegation for a small
group that desired to visit Perpignan several years ago. Marie worked as a Program
Officer for the World Bank in Paris specializing in Information Technology. She
holds BA & MA degrees in Romance Languages from the Univ. of Montpelier and
a Doctorate from the Sorbonne in Comparative Literature.

City Director Rapperswil-Jona Nelly Carmardo
Nelly is from Rapperswil-Jona and also served as the President of the Swiss
American Club of Sarasota. Her career has been in business and project
management and she worked for several years for the Bank of Canada. In Sarasota
she was the Customer Service Representative for the Sarasota Sailing Squadron.
Nelly has a BA teaching degree from the Tochterschule Zurich.

City Director Xiamen Douglas Sparks
Douglas earned his PhD in Anthropology from the University of Texas at Austin
with a focus on China and later obtained an MBA as well as completing graduate
work in computer science. He held senior technology leadership roles in global
companies in France, China, Canada, South Africa, Ghana and Kenya. His primary
interests today are the comparative study of mysticism, reengaging with China and
relearning Mandarin, as well as duplicate bridge.

City Director Tel Mond Fred Bloom
Dr. Fred Bloom has helped coordinate the installation of the Embracing Our
Differences on the Sarasota Bay Front and assisted with many other SCAS
programs. He had a long-time practice as an MD allergist as well as a civic leader
in Sarasota for many years.

City Director Teviso Susanna Wriston
Susanna lived in Italy for 20 years and later established the Italia Dolce Vita travel
business in Sarasota specializing in tours to Italy. She worked for several
international corporations from fashion with the Benetton Group to automotive with
Suzuki and FIAT-GM (Johnson Controls). She holds a BA in International Political
Science from the Univ. of Padua and an MA in marketing.

City Director Vladimir Olga Pliner
Olga is from Russia and is trilingual in English, German and Russian. She
specialized in Business Development and Sales and Marketing Management. She is
employed as a Finance Mgr for the City of Sarasota/Van Wezel Performing Arts
Center. Olga also held positions in management and accounting with several firms
in Germany. She hold a BA in Special Education from the Moscow State
Pedagogical Univ. and an MBA from Hagen Univ. in Germany.

Assistant City Director of Busseto Kenney DeCamp
Kenney has served in numerous capacities with Sister Cities, including VP of
Sports and VP of Finance. He has served as Master of Ceremonies for many of our
recent galas. Kenney is a man of many talents and was as a special events organizer
and promoter in Chicago, including the Taste of Chicago. He also is a talented
"mime" entertainer.

Assistant City Director Perpignan Emile Langlois
Emile is a native of Paris and an alumnus of the Sorbonne and the Ecole Normale
Supérieure de Cachan. He received a Doctorate from the Univ. of Montpellier. He
was a Fulbright Scholar at Shippensburg Univ. in PA and later taught at Mt
Holyoke College in MA where he also was Chair of the Dept of French. He
subsequently became a Professor of French at Sweet Briar College in VA where he
directed a program for Junior Year students in France.

Assistant City Director Tel Mond Kim Shiental
Kim also served as VP for Temple Emanu-El and as the local president for ORT
America, the Jewish Genealogical Society and the Women's Division of the Jewish
Federation. She was twice awarded the most active Sarasota County School
volunteer. Kim has given several presentations about the history of Tel Mond to our
community and published a book, "Jews of Sarasota-Manatee."

Assistant City Director Tel Mond Alice Cotman
Alice is an independent Non-Profit Organization Management Professional. She
was part of the sister city signing ceremony delegation with Tel Mond in 1999. She
has assisted with the many delegation visits from Tel Mond including the Tel Mond
Dancers, Tel Mond Singers, and all the Young Playwrights festivals. Alice also has
a special interest in the performing arts as an actress.

Assistant City Director of Merida Mike Fehily
Mike was also the City Director of Merida from many years. He teaches Spanish at
the University of South Florida-Sarasota/Manatee and has hosted numerous student
groups to Merida. He has accumulated and maintained many contacts in Merida
over the years.

Assistant City Director Xiamen Larry Bennison
Larry worked for Chevron as a Caltex Petroleum Financial Manager and Director in
Hong Kong, Seoul, Singapore, Manila, Tokyo and Dallas Corp Office. He is a
veteran Military Sealift Command Captain and a member of the Sarasota World
Affairs Council. His B.S. is from Purdue and an MBA from Wharton.

Current and Former SCAS Alliance Members

Alliance members are very important to the functioning of SCAS. Members of these clubs, associations, schools and community institutions serve as additional volunteers to arrange and host visiting sister city delegations. The organizations also graciously receive our visitors and offer tours, hosting and even providing facilities for SCAS events and programs. A culturally relevant alliance is also critical for introduction of a new sister city to our association for gaining official approval. We are indebted to the many alliance members that have assisted SCAS in the past sixty years.

Alliance Francaise de Sarasota
Ausonian Society of Sarasota
Boys and Girls Club of Sarasota
Caledonian Club of Sarasota
Circus Sarasota/Sailor Circus
Economic Development Commission of Sarasota County
Florida Studio Theater
French-American Business Council of West Florida
Greater Sarasota Chamber of Commerce
Gulf Coast Italian Culture Society
Gulf Coast Chinese American Association
Island Village Montessori Charter School
Jewish Federation of Sarasota & Manatee
Latino Excellence of Sarasota
Mote Marine Laboratory
Ringling Museum of Art
Rotary Club of the Sarasota Keys
Sarasota Association of Realtors, Inc.
Sarasota Christian School
Sarasota Community Youth Development
Sarasota Italian Cultural Events
State College of Florida
University of Florida IFAS
Sarasota County Extension
University of South Florida
US China Peoples Friendship Association
Visit Sarasota County

Board of Directors – Detailed Job Descriptions

Executive Committee of the Board

President
- Serves as Chairman of the Board of Directors.
- Serves as an Officer of the Corporation in accordance with State of Florida incorporation requirements.
- Elected by the Board of Directors and holds office year to year.
- Responsible for the general supervision of the affairs of the Corporation and over its other officers.
- Signatory of all official documents and communications of the Association.
- Responsible for submitting a report to the Corporation of the business transacted during the past year at the annual general meeting (AGM) of the membership, together with a report of the general financial condition of the Corporation.
- Responsible for submission of articles about specific city interests and events for publication on SCAS web and social media sites, general media distribution and the SCAS newsletter.
- Entitled in an emergency to authorize expenditures not to exceed Five Hundred Dollars ($500.00) on any single item without approval of the Board of Directors.
- Ensure money handling procedures established by SCAS Treasurer is followed, including notification of President and Treasurer of all membership transactions
- Portfolio of responsibilities includes:
    1. Presiding at all meetings of the Executive Committee and the Board of Directors;
    2. If unable to preside due to absence or disability, ensure that these duties are performed by a vice President, the Secretary, or the Treasurer.
    3. Preparation and submission of annual Corporate report required by the State of Florida (Department of State) and City of Sarasota.
    4. Provides leadership to the Board of Directors, who sets policy and to whom the Chief Executive is accountable.
    5. Encourages Board's role in strategic planning
    6. Appoints the chairpersons of committees, in consultation with other Board members.
    7. Serves ex officio as a member of committees and attends their meetings when invited.

Treasurer

- Member of the Executive Committee of the Board of Directors; reports to the Board.
- Serves as an Officer of the Corporation in accordance with State of Florida incorporation requirements.
- Under Article VI, Section 1 of the By-laws, as an Officer, is elected by the Board of Directors at the annual meeting and holds office year to year.
- Custodian of the funds of the Corporation.
- Responsible for submission of articles about specific city interests and events for publication on SCAS web and social media sites, general media distribution and the SCAS newsletter.
- Establish money handling procedures to be followed by all board members.
- Portfolio of responsibilities includes:
    1. Keeping regular books and accounts in accordance with GAAP, together with vouchers, receipts, records and other papers normally incident to this office, and making these records available to the Board or their authorized representatives at reasonable times;
    2. Ensuring that checks in an amount exceeding Five Hundred Dollars ($500.00) are signed by two officers of the Board;
    3. Providing timely reports on the financial status of the Corporation to the Board of Directors;
    4. With input from the Board, developing an annual Budget for the Corporation, and monitoring its status throughout the fiscal year.
    5. Prepare documentation necessary for submission of annual Federal Income Tax forms, plus fulfilling State of Florida Corporate, Sales Tax Exemption and Charity reporting requirements.

Vice President – Business & Economic Development

- Member of the Executive Committee of the Board of Directors; reports to the Board.
- Under Article VI of the By-laws, is elected by the Board of Directors at the annual meeting and holds office year to year.
- Responsible for submission of articles about specific city interests and events for publication on SCAS web and social media sites, general media distribution and the SCAS newsletter.
- Ensure money handling procedures established by SCAS Treasurer are followed, including notification of the President and Treasurer of all membership transactions.
- Portfolio of responsibilities includes:
    1. Strengthening people-to-people relations between sister cities, through involvement of Cultural Coast businesses and those in our sister cities.
    2. Keeping informed about the business climate of the community with

special emphasis on identifying partnership opportunities for individual sister cities and for SCAS;
3. Identifying and developing opportunities to make business leaders aware of the possibilities for value-added relationships with SCAS and its member sister cities.
4. Keep Economic Development Info on sarasotasistercities.com

Vice President - Cities & Candidate Cities

- Member of the Executive Committee of the Board of Directors; reports to the Board.
- Serves as an Officer of the Corporation in accordance with State of Florida incorporation requirements.
- Under Article VI of the By-laws, as an Officer, is elected by the Board of Directors at the annual meeting and holds office year to year.
- Responsible for acting as liaison between the City Directors (CDs) and the Executive Committee.
- Responsible for submission of articles about specific city interests and events for publication on SCAS web and social media sites, general media distribution and the SCAS newsletter.
- Ensure money handling procedures established by SCAS Treasurer are followed, including notification of the President and Treasurer of all membership transactions.
- Portfolio of responsibilities includes:
  1. Coordinating activities among CDs;
  2. Helping CDs to identify resources with and outside of the organization;
  3. Acting in an advisory capacity in the development and management of CD's individual city committees.
- Oversees the process of evaluating prospective candidate cities to ensure that Board-approved criteria for selection are adhered to.
- Assists prospective sister cities to appreciate the obligations of both candidate and full-status sister cities.
- Makes recommendations to the Executive committee and the Board with regard to the admissibility of applicant sister cities.

Vice President - Communications

- Member of the Executive Committee of the Board of Directors; reports to the Board.
- Under Article VI of the By-laws, is elected by the Board of Directors at the annual meeting and holds office year to year.
- Responsible for developing and implementing SCAS's communications plan.
- Responsible for submission of articles about specific city interests and events for publication on SCAS web and social media sites, general media
The Communication Team

- distribution and the SCAS newsletter.
- Sets up and maintains the Sarasota Sister Cities email system, Sister City Blog, Facebook page, Twitter account, LinkedIn account, and Pinterest pages.
- Blog: http://sarasotasistercities.com
- Ensure money handling procedures established by SCAS Treasurer are followed, including notification of the President and Treasurer of all membership transactions.
- Portfolio of responsibilities includes:
  1. Ensuring that SCAS's message to the community is clear, consistent, and effectively communicated;
  2. Seeking opportunities for public exposure of SCAS and its projects in print, electronic and social media;
  3. Planning the design and content of a SCAS marketing and communication package.
  4. Acts in an advisory and oversight capacity for the SCAS Newsletter Blog, its design, writing, and production.
  5. Acts in an advisory and oversight capacity for the SCAS Website, its development, content, and maintenance.
  6. Acts in an advisory and oversight capacity for special events, ensuring that clear objectives have been identified, and that an effective communications plan is in place.
  7. Responsible for submission of articles about specific city interests and events for publication on SCAS web and social media sites, general media distribution and the SCAS newsletter.
  8. Assists in the planning and promotion of members' luncheons.

Vice President – Arts & Culture
- Member of the Executive Committee of the Board of Directors; reports to the Board.
- Under Article VI of the By-laws, is elected by the Board of Directors at the annual meeting and holds office year to year.
- Responsible for developing and nurturing contacts with leaders in the cultural sector: museums, galleries, schools of art, theatre, film, the Arts Council, and others as appropriate.
- Responsible for planning and implementing SCAS Board-approved projects and special initiatives in the areas of culture; and for developing and nurturing relationships between cultural institutions and SCAS, in order to identify and promote partnership opportunities.
- Responsible for submission of articles about specific city interests and events for publication on SCAS web and social media sites, general media distribution and the SCAS newsletter.
- Portfolio of responsibilities includes:
  1. Holding regular meetings with leaders in the
  2. various areas of the cultural sector to identify opportunities for

collaboration with one or more of our sister cities;
3. Analyzing and recommending collaborative projects for consideration, including the budgetary implications of such projects;
4. Facilitating and evaluating approved projects;
5. Acts in an advisory and oversight capacity for the City Directors and event chairs, being a resource for those who plan individual cultural projects.

Vice President - Education

- Member of the Executive Committee of the Board of Directors; reports to the Board.
- Under Article VI of the By-laws, is elected by the Board of Directors at the annual meeting and holds office year to year.
- Responsible for planning and implementing SCAS Board-approved projects and special initiatives in the area of education;
- Develops and nurtures relationships between educational institutions and SCAS, in order to identify and promote partnership opportunities.
- Ensure money handling procedures established by SCAS Treasurer are followed, including notification of the President and Treasurer of all membership transactions.
- Responsible for submission of articles about specific city interests and events for publication on SCAS web and social media sites, general media distribution and the SCAS newsletter.
- Portfolio of responsibilities includes:
    1. Overseeing and planning SCAS educational projects to ensure that:
        a) Project objectives have been clearly defined;
        b) A sound budget has been developed and sources of financing identified;
        a) Assisting the VP for Communications in creating event marketing and communications plans;
    2. Overseeing the implementation of projects, and monitoring their progress.
- Acts in an advisory capacity to the Community Youth Department appointed member to the SCAS Executive Board, filling the Youth Ambassador position.
- Acts as a resource for City Directors who plan individual educational projects.

Vice President – Fundraising

- Member of the Executive Committee of the Board of Directors; reports to the Board.
- Under Article VI of the By-laws, is elected by the Board of Directors at the annual meeting and holds office year to year.
- Responsible for developing an active program to obtain donations and grants to assist the organization in meeting established goals and unfunded

initiatives of the organization.
- Acts as a resource and advisor for identifying possible sources for donation or grant support for City Directors who plan unfunded events and have established defendable budget requirements.
- Responsible for submission of articles about specific city interests and events for publication on SCAS web and social media sites, general media distribution and the SCAS newsletter.
- Ensure money handling procedures established by SCAS Treasurer are followed, including notification of the President and Treasurer of all membership transactions.

Vice President – Membership
- Member of the Executive Committee of the Board of Directors; reports to the Board.
- Under Article VI of the By-laws, is elected by the Board of Directors at the annual meeting and holds office year to year.
- Responsible for maintaining the current SCAS membership database, alliance member database, including electronic and non-electronic contact with membership records.
- Responsible for submission of articles about specific city interests and events for publication on SCAS web and social media sites, general media distribution and the SCAS newsletter.
- Ensure money handling procedures established by SCAS Treasurer are followed, including notification of the President and Treasurer of all membership transactions.
- Responsible for developing and implementing SCAS's membership outreach planning.
- Responsible for reviewing written Alliance membership nominations for completeness; evaluating whether the nomination meets SCAS criteria; and referring the nomination to the Executive Committee with a rationale for recommending acceptance or rejection of the nomination.
- Portfolio of responsibilities includes:
    1. Create a welcome letter and a new member handbook to be provided electronically or by mail to new members. Solicit interests of new members as a follow-up to welcome and handbook distribution.
    2. Notify board members, including city directors, of names and interests of all new members.
    3. Acts in an advisory capacity for special events, ensuring membership outreach initiatives have been identified.

Vice President - Sports
- Member of the Executive Committee of the Board of Directors; reports to the Board.
- Under Article VI of the By-laws, is elected by the Board of Directors at the annual meeting and holds office year to year.

- Responsible for planning and implementing SCAS Board-approved projects and special initiatives in the area of sports events and exchanges.
- Ensure money handling procedures established by SCAS Treasurer are followed, including notification of the President and Treasurer of all membership transactions.
- Responsible for submission of articles about specific city interests and events for publication on SCAS web and social media sites, general media distribution and the SCAS newsletter.
- Portfolio of responsibilities includes:
    1. Identifying opportunities for individual and team sport projects in Sarasota aimed at involving our sister cities; (e.g., tournaments; camps, etc.)
    2. Identifying opportunities for individual and team sport exchanges between Sarasota and our sister cities;
    3. Ensuring that proposals put forward by CDs are well-thought out as to logistics, budget, timeframes and resources, etc.
    4. Serving as a resource for City Directors regarding opportunities for sports exchanges.

Vice President of Events
- Member of the Executive Committee of the Board of Directors; reports to the Board.
- Under Article VI of the By-laws, is elected by the Board of Directors at the annual meeting and holds office year to year.
- Responsible for planning and implementing SCAS Board-approved events.
- Responsible for coordinating monthly members' luncheons and other members' special events.
- Portfolio of responsibilities includes:
    1. Booking the venue where the luncheon/event will take place;
    2. Determining the menu, in consultation with the originator;
    3. Collecting money for and recording reservations;
    4. Creating name tags and place cards, as appropriate for each event;
    5. Coordinating volunteers to greet guests and staff reservation tables.

City Director
- Reports to the Vice President, Cities & Candidate Cities.
- Member of the Board of Directors.
- Elected by the Membership for a two-year term of office; reelection shall be for a term of one year.
- Responsible for managing and enhancing the relationship between SCAS and the individual sister city.
- Ensure money handling procedures established by SCAS Treasurer are followed, including notification of the President and Treasurer of all membership transactions.
- Responsible for submission of articles about specific city interests and

events for publication on SCAS web and social media sites, general media distribution and the SCAS newsletter.
- Portfolio of other responsibilities includes:
    1. Maintaining verbal, electronic, and written communications with the individual sister city;
    2. Chairing a sister city committee representative of local volunteers and volunteer associations;
    3. Identifying opportunities for collaboration between SCAS and the sister city, and/or among a group of sister cities;
    4. Facilitating periodic exchanges between the sister city and Sarasota;
    5. Bringing forward recommendations for projects suggested by the sister city;
    6. Developing and submitting to the Board an annual budget;
    7. Specifying budgetary implications for proposed projects before they are undertaken;
    8. Building awareness on the part of the Board and general membership about the special characteristics of the individual sister city through web presence, presentations, articles for publication, and use of our social media sites.
    9. Evaluating the individual sister city relationship on an annual basis.

Youth Ambassador
- Reports to the Vice President - Education
- Appointed annually to be a member of the Executive Board by the Alliance member Sarasota County Youth Development organization.
- Responsible for representing the views and interest of youth on the Board of Directors.
- Ensure money handling procedures established by SCAS Treasurer are followed, including notification of the President and Treasurer of all membership transactions.
- Responsible for submission of articles about youth interests and events for publication on SCAS web and social media sites, general media distribution and the SCAS newsletter.
- Portfolio of responsibilities includes:
    1. Becoming knowledgeable about how not-for-profit Boards function;
    2. Bringing forward opportunities for SCAS involvement in youth initiatives;
    3. Carrying through on projects assigned by the Board, with the view to increasing awareness and expertise in aspects of not-for-profit management.
    4. Being project manager for use of SCAS Facebook & Twitter outreach to youth in the Cultural Coast and our sister cities, in coordination with the VPs for Communications. Education and Membership.

Assistant City Directors & Special Contributors
(Non-voting members of the Board)

Assistant City Director
- Nominated by the City Director and approved by the President.
- Non-voting member of the Board of Directors.
- Reports to the City Director.
- Responsible for assisting in the management of the relationship between SCAS and the individual sister city.
- Responsible for submission of articles about specific city interests and events for publication on SCAS web and social media sites, general media distribution and the SCAS newsletter.
- Portfolio of responsibilities includes:
    1. Helping to maintain verbal, electronic, and written communications with the individual sister city;
    2. Assisting in chairing the sister city committee of local volunteers and volunteer associations;
    3. Helping to identify opportunities for collaboration between SCAS and the sister city;
    4. Assisting in facilitating periodic exchanges between the sister city and Sarasota;
    5. Helping to promote the sister city through presentations, articles in the newsletter, and other forms of communication, etc.
    6. Assisting in the management of specific projects as assigned by the City Director.

Protocol Advisor
- Reports to, and is appointed by, the President.
- Non-voting member of the Board of Directors.
- Responsible for ensuring that Board Members and others associated with SCAS are aware of the protocol requirements for international and national delegations.
- Portfolio of responsibilities includes:
    1. Familiarity with the Florida League of Cities International Relations Protocol book and other recognized protocol guidelines;
    2. Researching the specific protocol requirements for foreign delegations and for SCAS foreign visitations;
    3. Briefing city directors and other members of SCAS Board on the proper protocol for the city or country in question for visitations and foreign delegations;
    4. Developing a list of appropriate official gifts for foreign dignitaries;
    5. Recommending appropriate gifts that reflect the seniority of the recipient vis á vis his or her subordinates;
    6. Developing and maintaining a Gift Log, to avoid duplications and inappropriate gifts (i.e., gifts already given to a subordinate, etc.).

Grant Writer
- Appointed by the Vice President – Fundraising.
- Reports to the VP for FundRaising.
- Non-voting member of the Board of Directors.
- Responsible for identifying traditional and crowd giving funding opportunities for SCAS projects, writing proposals to obtain funds, and providing follow-up with funders.
- Portfolio of responsibilities includes:
    1. Assisting city directors in selection of well-thought-out cases for support;
    2. Identifying appropriate funding sources for specific projects;
    3. Maintaining the SCAS file of documents required for grant submissions required by Guide Star, Florida Department of Agriculture (CH Forms) and Community Foundations.
    4. Ensuring that required documentation is submitted with grant proposals, including project budgets;
    5. Ensuring that all fiduciary, reporting, and recognition requirements are adhered to;
    6. Maintaining contact with relevant funding sources and promoting SCAS interests, per direction of the VP for Fund Raising.

Newsletter Editor
Sarasota Sister Cities publishes an online Newsletter. The Newsletter can be found at sarasotasistercities.org.
- Appointed by, and reports to, the VP for Communications. (currently is the VP of communications
- Non-voting member of the Board of Directors.
- Responsible for editing and production of the SCAS Newsletter Blog.
- Portfolio of responsibilities includes:
    1. Collecting content from Board members and other sources
    2. Obtaining approval from SCAS President or VP for Communication
    3. Overseeing the newsletter production and distribution process.

Volunteers Welcomed

Sarasota Sister Cities Needs a Few Good People

Please let us know if you would like to volunteer services to Sarasota Sister Cities. Positions come up periodically. We also need assistance with programs targeted for a specific Sister Cities. Please let us know if you have an interest in working with our sister cities in China, France, Israel, Italy, Mexico, Switzerland, Russia, or Scotland.

We welcome your help for any position on the Board. You can volunteer to help one of our officers in a field of your interest. This is a great way to not only help SCAS, but to get to know people, and to eventually move on to a Board position. Email us if you would like to help out and we will put you in touch with the right person.

SCAS Office Address:
111 S. Orange St, Suite 103
Sarasota, FL 34236

SCAS Mailing Address:
P.O. Box 674
Sarasota, FL 34230

Website: sarasotasistercities.org
E-mail: sarasotasistercities@gmail.com

Conclusion

Sarasota Sister Cities Association has followed and continued on the mission of promoting Peace and Understanding in the World through the plethora of exchange programs with sister cities and the many community programs and events offered in the past sixty years. SCAS has created many international relationships through citizen diplomacy, that is, People-to-People exchanges.

The organization has expanded Cultural, Educational, Governmental and Professional horizons for sister city members both in Sarasota and sister cities as well as many in the Sarasota community in general. We are proud of the work we have done and the accomplishments towards better understanding in the world.

Links and References

General Links

Web	sarasotasistercities.org
Facebook	facebook.com/SarasotaSisterCities
Pinterest	pinterst.com/sarasotasister
Twitter	twitter.com/#!/SarasotaSisterC
Email	**sarasotasistercities@gmail.com**
Newsletters	bridgestotheworldssc.blogspot.com

Sister City Blogs

bussetosarasota.blogspot.com
dunfermlinesarasota.blogspot.com
hamiltonsarasota.blogspot.com
meridasarasota.blogspot.com
perpignansarasota.blogspot.com
rapperswil-jona.sarasota.blogspot.com
telmondsarasota.blogspot.com
vladimirsarasota.blogspot.com
xiamensarasota.blogspot.com

History

historysarasota.blogspot.com

Communication & Newsletters

videos sarasota.blogspot.com
sistercitiessocialmarketing.blogspot.com
socialnetworkingreport.blogspot.com
eventssarasotasister.blogspot
Newsletters: Bridgestotheworldssc.blogspot.com

Photos

photossarasota.blogspot.com
bigphotossarasota.blogspot.com
galaobserversarasota.blogspot.com

Sustainable Development

sarasotasistercites.com
sarasotasistercities.blogspot.com
animationsarasota.blogspot.com
economicdevelopmentreports.blogspot.com
greensarasota.blogspot.com

sustainablesarasota.blogspot.com
sarasotasistercitiesdevelopment.blogspot.com
sarasotatownsquare.blogspot.com
sarasotacityplanning.blogspot.com

Videos

You-Tube presentation videos (URLs) that describe our SCAS organization and our Sister Cities. The videos run 10-15 min each. <u>Videos also online at:</u> <u>https//videossarasotasistercities.blogspot.com/2023/11/sister-cities-videos</u>

SCAS Part I – <u>Selection of Sister Cities and Administration</u>
    https://youtu.be/qt5k3X2Gx1Y?si=mOgzlWPy4wTFIULi
SCAS Part II – <u>Innovation Awards & Sister Cities Perpignan & Tel Mond</u>
    https://youtu.be/4_M8jEoMlLY?si=ruXRGJKoO5CJc0Dp
SCAS Part III – <u>Sister Cities Dunfermline & Xiamen</u>
    https://youtu.be/1qblQd5ttmg?si=w-AEbpeeNpZVD3Fi
SCAS Part IV – <u>Sister Cities Treviso, Merida, Vladimir & Rapperswil-Jona</u>
    https://youtu.be/lOeXFKCgOF0?si=WD5xxF8qWfqCEb33
SCAS Part V – <u>Community Activities of SCAS</u>
    https://youtu.be/18QNESBvdhs?si=8Xjmi0ti-MX-GOhQ

Tel Mond Sister City Song

sistercitysongs.blogspot.com

Micellaneous

sistercitysongs.blogspot.com
birdsofsarasota.blogspot.com
sunsetsarasotablogspot.com
sscnewsletter.blogspot.com
policydocuments.blogspot.com
sscitiesnew.blogspot.com
sscgraphic.blogspot.com
warandpeacesarasota.blogspot.com

References

en.wikipedia.org/wiki/Busseto
en.wikipedia.org/wiki/Dunfermline
en.wikipedia.org/wiki/Merida
en.wikipedia.org/wiki/Perpignan
en.wikipedia.org/wiki/Provence_of_Treviso
en.wikipedia.org/wiki/Rapperswil
en.wikipedia.org/wiki/Santo_Domingo
en.wikipedia.org/wiki/Xiamen

About the Authors

 **Craig H. Hullinger**

Craig Hullinger served many years on the SCAS Board of Directors as Vice President of Communication and later as Vice President of Economic Development. He developed many of the social media sites and blogs for SCAS. Craig is from Illinois and was a County Planning Director, Village Manager, City Economic Development Director and City Planning and Economic Development Consultant. He is a Vietnam Veteran and a retired Marine Colonel. He has a BA in Government and an MA in Planning. Craighullinger.com, https://planningnews.blogspot.com.

 **Raymond A. Young**

Raymond Young served on the SCAS Board of Directors for 15 years as Vice President of Education and later as Vice President of Programs and Planning. He is an Emeritus Professor at the University of Wisconsin-Madison where he taught and carried our research on biomaterials for 30 years. His international experience included a year as a Fulbright graduate student at the Royal Inst. of Technology in Stockholm, Sweden and a year at the Aristotelian Univ. in Thessaloniki, Greece as a Senior Fulbright Scholar. He also was employed as a Process Supervisor in fine paper production for the Kimberly-Clark Corp in Niagara Fall, NY for one year. His B.S. & M.S. are from Syracuse Univ. and PhD from the Univ. of Washington. www.researchgate.net/profile/RA_Young.